# PRACTICE
# MAKES
# PERFECT

# *Advanced*
# Spanish
# Grammar

**Rogelio Alonso Vallecillos**

New York   Chicago   San Francisco   Lisbon   London   Madrid   Mexico City
Milan   New Delhi   San Juan   Seoul   Singapore   Sydney   Toronto

Copyright © 2008 by The McGraw-Hill Companies, Inc. All rights reserved. Printed in the
United States of America. Except as permitted under the United States Copyright Act of
1976, no part of this publication may be reproduced or distributed in any form or by any
means, or stored in a database or retrieval system, without the prior written permission of
the publisher.

1  2  3  4  5  6  7  8  9  10  11  12  13  14  15  16  17  18  19  20  21    FGR/FGR    0  9  8

ISBN 978-0-07-147268-5
MHID     0-07-147268-1
Library of Congress Control Number: 2006939544

Interior design by Village Typographers, Inc.

McGraw-Hill books are available at special quantity discounts to use as premiums and
sales promotions or for use in corporate training programs. To contact a representative,
please visit the Contact Us pages at www.mhprofessional.com.

This book is printed on acid-free paper.

# Contents

Introduction  v

**1**  Object pronouns and omission of subject pronouns  1

**2**  *Some/any* and other determiners  17

**3**  Adjectives  32

**4**  Adverbs  50

**5**  Commands and requests  76

**6**  Modal constructions  88

**7**  Impersonal sentences and the passive  101

**8**  Relative pronouns and conjunctions  113

**9**  Reported speech  130

**10**  Problematic prepositions I  149

**11**  Problematic prepositions II  162

**12**  Idiomatic constructions  176

Answer key  193

# Introduction

This book provides the necessary tools to make your speech and writing in Spanish much more *Spanish*. It deals with topics that often cause trouble to foreign students, especially to English-speaking ones: topics like the correct use of object pronouns, when to leave out subject pronouns, how to generate sentences that indicate proposal, suggestion, reproach, and so on. The book also deals with the creation of impersonal sentences, passive constructions, and reported speech. Its units on adjectives and adverbs, as well as other items covered, will help English-speaking students avoid common mistakes. The thorough explanations on relative pronouns and conjunctions will enable you to create longer and much more interesting sentences. Finally, the book offers a varied selection of idioms that will make your speech sound absolutely Spanish.

In each unit you will find thorough explanations of the grammar at hand, including numerous examples that illustrate and clarify each point. Along the way, boxed inserts provide further information and offer tips or guidance on usage. At the end of each unit are several, varied practice exercises that will give you a comprehensive grasp of everything that has been covered in the unit. The answer key even includes extra explanations for the trickier questions. You can either work through the book from beginning to end or dip in and out of particular chapters of interest. By the time you have gone through the book, your Spanish will be much closer to a native speaker's.

**¡Suerte!**

# Object pronouns and omission of subject pronouns

·1·

Most students of Spanish know that Spanish subject pronouns (**yo**, **tú**, **ella**, and so on) can often be omitted, because they are usually not necessary for comprehension—that is, it is clear from the verb form which grammatical person is meant. But there are cases in which their use is compulsory and cases in which their use or omission hides important nuances. Another important aspect of Spanish grammar is the correct use of object pronouns, which can be troublesome even to Spanish speakers. Why a sentence like **A ella la dieron el dinero** (very common in central Spain) is incorrect is one of the problems that this unit will address.

## Object pronouns

Object pronouns can cause difficulties to learners of Spanish, especially third-person forms, because their use depends on their grammatical function. This section will deal with general aspects of object pronouns and with third-person forms in their different functions.

## General information

There are two different groups of object pronouns, those that are preceded by prepositions and those that are not. When no prepositions are used, the Spanish object pronouns are:

| | | | |
|---|---|---|---|
| **me** | *me* | **lo/la/le** | *it* |
| **te** | *you* (informal singular) | **nos** | *us* |
| **le/lo** | *him* | **os** | *you* (formal plural) |
| **le/la** | *her* | **les/las/los** | *them* |

1

With **usted** and **ustedes**, third-person forms (**le/la/lo/les/las/los**) must be used.

These pronouns are placed before a conjugated verb. If there is an infinitive or a gerund in the verb sequence, they can be put after the infinitive or after the gerund as well (without a space):

| | |
|---|---|
| Yo **le** veo. | *I see him.* |
| **Lo** necesito. | *I need it.* |
| **Les** quiero ver. (O: Quiero ver**les**.) | *I want to see them.* |
| **Lo** estoy estudiando. | *I am studying it.* |
| (O: Estoy estudiándo**lo**.) | |

The accent appears because words with stress that is not on the next-to-the-last syllable must always take an accent (**estudiándolo**).

With prepositions, the following pronouns must be used:

| | |
|---|---|
| **mí** (with an accent) | *me* |
| **ti** (without an accent) | *you* (singular and informal) |
| **usted** | *you* (singular and formal) |
| **él** | *him/it* |
| **ella** | *her/it* |
| **ello** | *it* |
| **nosotros/nosotras** | *us* |
| **vosotros/vosotras** | *you* (plural and informal) |
| **ustedes** | *you* (plural and formal) |
| **ellos/ellas** | *them* |

The preposition **con** (*with*) combines with **mí** to form **conmigo** and with **ti** to form **contigo**:

| | |
|---|---|
| No puedo hacer esto **sin ti**. | *I can't do this without you.* |
| Ella quiere hablar **contigo**. | *She wants to talk with you.* |
| Esa carta es **para mí**. | *That letter is for me.* |
| Ellos van a trabajar **conmigo**. | *They are going to work with me.* |
| Ella no puede vivir **con él**. | *She can't live with him.* |
| Este regalo es **para ella**. | *This present is for her.* |

The use of the neuter object pronoun **ello** is confined to formal language. It can never refer to animals or things (including abstract entities) because nouns in Spanish are either masculine or feminine, never neuter. **Ello** can only be used to refer to a context or to an action mentioned before:

| | |
|---|---|
| Ana: ¿Tienes el informe final? | *Do you have the final report?* |
| Carlos: No, estoy trabajando en **ello**. | *No, I'm working on it.* |

In this example, **ello** refers to the fact that Carlos has to finish the report, not to the report itself. If the reference were to the report, **él** would be used (**informe** is masculine, not neuter).

# Use of third-person object pronouns

Without prepositions, third-person object pronouns are a little difficult to use, as their use depends on whether they are direct or indirect objects. When the object pronoun is the direct object of the sentence, either **le** or **lo** can be used if the pronoun refers to a masculine singular human being. Only **lo** is possible if it refers to a masculine animal or object:

| | |
|---|---|
| **Le/Lo** voy a ver. | *I am going to see him.* |
| **Lo** voy a comprar (coche). | *I am going to buy it (car).* |

The same rule applies to plural masculine pronouns when they are the direct objects of a sentence:

| | |
|---|---|
| **Les/Los** voy a invitar. | *I am going to invite them (people).* |
| **Los** voy a vender. | *I am going to sell them (paintings, perhaps).* |

Only **lo** is possible when it refers to a context, preceding information, and so on:

| | |
|---|---|
| Pepe: ¿Sabes que el presidente nos va a visitar? | *Do you know that the president is going to visit us?* |
| Luis: Sí, **lo** leí ayer en el periódico. | *Yes, I read it (about it) in the newspaper yesterday.* |

When the pronoun refers to a feminine direct object (human or not), **la** must be used in the singular and **las** in the plural, never **los/les**:

| | |
|---|---|
| **La** voy a pintar (cocina). | *I am going to paint it (kitchen).* |
| No **la** necesito (enfermera). | *I don't need her (nurse).* |

**Enfermera** and **cocina** are feminine words.

When the pronoun is the indirect object of the sentence, **le** is always used in the singular and **les** in the plural, whether it refers to a human being or not, masculine or feminine:

| | |
|---|---|
| **Le** voy a dar agua. | *I am going to give him/her/it some water.* |
| **Les** voy a dar comida. | *I am going to give them some food.* |

When it is not clear who or what the pronoun is referring to, **a** + subject pronoun/noun can be added (the object pronoun remains):

| | |
|---|---|
| **Le** voy a dar agua **a ella**. | *I am going to give water to her.* |
| **Le** voy a dar agua **a la niña**. | *I am going to give water to the girl (or: give the girl water).* |

This "double use" of object pronoun and **a** + pronoun/noun in the same sequence is compulsory when the pronoun is the indirect object. When the pronoun is the direct object, double use occurs as well, but the preposition **a** can only be followed by a pronoun, never by a noun. This rule is applicable to all object pronouns:

| | |
|---|---|
| **Le** tengo que decir **a Elena** que... | *I have to tell Elena that . . .* |
| **Os** tengo que decir **a vosotros** que... | *I have to tell you that . . .* |
| **Te** voy a dar esto **a ti**. | *I'm going to give this to you.* |
| No **la** puedo ver **a ella**, sino a él. | *I can't see her, but him.* |

A sentence like **No la puedo ver a Elena** is incorrect, as double use is not possible with nouns that function as direct objects.

An exception occurs when the direct object is placed at the beginning of a sentence. Double use is then compulsory. Compare:

| | |
|---|---|
| No voy a llamar **a Mari**. | *I'm not going to phone Mari.* |
| **A Mari** no **la** voy a llamar. | *I'm not going to phone Mari.* |

In sentences where the direct object is represented by an object pronoun, third-person pronouns functioning as indirect objects are replaced by the reflexive pronoun **se**:

| | |
|---|---|
| **Se lo** voy a dar (a ellos). | *I am going to give it to them.* |
| **Se la** voy a dar (a ella). | *I am going to give it to her.* |

In such cases, the direct object is represented by the pronouns **lo**, **la**, **los**, and **las** (never **le** or **les**), depending on the gender and number of the "object" represented by the pronoun. This is applicable to the other grammatical persons:

| | |
|---|---|
| Ella **me lo** va a prestar. | *She is going to lend it to me.* |
| Yo no **te las** voy a dar. | *I am not going to give them to you.* |

The rule is actually very simple. Third-person pronouns can't appear together to represent the direct and the indirect objects. In such cases, the indirect object is always **se**, which is always mentioned first. In the sentence *I explained it to them*, *it* is the direct object and *them* is the indirect object. *Them* is translated as **se**. The pronoun *it* is translated as **lo** or **la**, depending on the gender of the word represented by *it*. With **se**, the pronouns **le** and **les** can't be used:

<table>
<tr><td>Ana **se lo** va a traer (a él).</td><td>*Ana is going to bring it to him.*</td></tr>
<tr><td>Yo **se los** tengo que devolver (a ellos).</td><td>*I have to give them back to them.*</td></tr>
</table>

The context usually makes it clear who **se** refers to. If not, a clause with **a** + noun/pronoun is added:

<table>
<tr><td>Yo **se la** presté a tu hermano.</td><td>*I lent it to your brother.*</td></tr>
</table>

Gerunds and infinitives can be followed by a direct and an indirect object pronoun (without a space between them):

<table>
<tr><td>Yo voy a dár**telos**.</td><td>*I am going to give them to you.*</td></tr>
<tr><td>Ella está dándo**mela**.</td><td>*She is giving it to me.*</td></tr>
<tr><td>Tienes que dár**selo**.</td><td>*You have to give it to him/her/them.*</td></tr>
</table>

With **usted/ustedes**, **le/lo** and **les/los** are used when the pronoun is the direct object and refers to masculine people. **La** and **las** are used when the pronoun is the direct object and refers to feminine people. When the pronoun is the indirect object, only **le** and **les** are possible:

<table>
<tr><td>Yo no **la** voy a invitar a usted.</td><td>*I'm not going to invite you (to a woman).*</td></tr>
<tr><td>Yo a usted no **le/lo** quiero ver aquí.</td><td>*I don't want to see you here (to a man).*</td></tr>
<tr><td>Yo a usted **le** voy a dar una sorpresa.</td><td>*I am going to give you a surprise (to a man or woman).*</td></tr>
</table>

The phrase with **a** can be omitted.

## Object pronouns with **gustar** and similar verbs

Many verbs that express liking and disliking in their different aspects have to be preceded by object pronouns. In general, these verbs are those that provoke a change in the speaker's personal attitude/feelings toward something. Some important examples are **aterrar** (*terrify*), **encantar** (*love*), **gustar** (*like*), **disgustar** (*dislike*), and so on.

<table>
<tr><td>**A mí me** encanta levantarme temprano.</td><td>*I love getting up early.*</td></tr>
<tr><td>**A Antonio** no **le** gusta la cerveza.</td><td>*Antonio doesn't like beer.*</td></tr>
</table>

With these verbs, the third-person pronouns **lo**, **la**, **los**, and **las** can't be used. Only **le** and **les** are possible. A sentence like **A ella la gusta el vino** is incorrect. You must say **A ella le gusta el vino** (*She likes wine*).

Conjugated forms of these verbs can't be followed by object pronouns in Spanish. A sentence like *I like them* has to be translated by **Me gustan** (with the verb in its plural third-person form). The context usually makes it clear who or what the speaker is referring to.

# Omission of subject pronouns

You have already noticed that subject pronouns are often left out in Spanish. This can be done because most grammatical persons have a different verb form. As a result of this, subject pronouns are generally not necessary to clarify who or what the verb refers to. The English form *are*, for example, goes with *you, we,* and *they*. But in Spanish, each of these grammatical persons has a different verb form (**eres, somos,** and **son**), which makes it possible to leave out the subject pronoun without creating confusion. Despite this, there are cases in which it is advisable or even compulsory to use them.

## Omission of ello

The neuter subject pronoun **ello** can be used only to refer to a context or situation, never to an animal or thing, and certainly not to people. People, animals, and things (including abstract nouns) have either a masculine or a feminine gender; they are never neuter. The demonstrative pronoun **eso** may be used instead of a subject that refers to a context or situation or the subject may be left out:

| | |
|---|---|
| No debes tocar los cables, porque (eso) es peligroso. | *You mustn't touch the cables because it's/that's dangerous.* |
| Marta aprobó todos los exámenes. ¿No es (eso) sorprendente? | *Marta passed all the exams. Isn't it/that amazing?* |

**Eso** can't be used when the sequence is followed by an infinitive or a clause with a relative pronoun. Omission of the subject is then compulsory:

| | |
|---|---|
| Es peligroso tocar esos cables. | *It's dangerous to touch those cables.* |
| Es sorprendente que ella... | *It's amazing that she . . .* |

Subject pronouns are never used in a sentence like **¿Qué es?** (*What is it?*) They are either omitted or the demonstratives **esto** and **eso** are used: **¿Qué es esto/eso?** (*What is this/that?*) These neuter demonstratives are very common when explaining what something is (for plural as well as singular nouns). If the noun used is preceded by determiners (articles, possessives, etc.), **esto** and **eso** can't be used. Compare:

| | |
|---|---|
| **Esto** son libretas, no libros. | *These/They are notebooks, not books.* |
| **Éstas** son mis libretas. | *These are my notebooks.* |

**Ello** is often used as an object pronoun, in sentences of the type **Estoy trabajando en ello** (*I'm working on it*). In this kind of sentence, **ello** refers to the whole action mentioned before, not to a particular object:

| | |
|---|---|
| Marta: ¿Están listos los ejercicios? | *Are the exercises ready?* |
| Pablo: Estoy trabajando en **ello**. | *I'm working on it.* |

If Pablo referred to the exercises, he would have to say **en ellos**. The gerund **trabajando** can be left out (**Estoy en ello**).

## Omission of other subject pronouns

When referring to things, Spanish-speaking people usually leave out the subject pronoun or repeat the name of the thing talked about:

| | |
|---|---|
| ¿A qué hora abren las tiendas? | *What time do the shops open?* |
| Abren a las cinco. | *They open at five o'clock.* |
| (O: Las tiendas abren a las cinco.) | *(Or: The stores open at five o'clock.)* |

When referring to a table, for example, a sentence like **Ella es de madera** is highly unusual. The subject pronoun is used only when the speaker needs or wants to be emphatic or very specific.

In talking about animals, the use of subject pronouns is a little more frequent, especially with animals that belong to the speaker's domestic environment and with larger wild animals (mainly mammals). In talking about a she-cat, for example, **Ella es la madre de esos gatitos** (*She is the mother of those little kittens*) sounds correct, but **Ella está en el jardín** (*She is in the garden*) sounds a little strange, unless it is said by somebody who adores cats and personifies them.

In conversation, the speaker who first introduces a subject doesn't need to use the subject pronoun, but other speakers do use it when they go on talking about the same subject (often using the same verb):

| | |
|---|---|
| Juan: (Yo) Soy médico. | *I am a doctor.* |
| Pablo: Yo soy arquitecto. | *I am an architect.* |

Juan doesn't have to use the subject pronoun, but Pablo must use it as he is reacting to Juan's words using the same verb.

When a speaker asks someone a question, the second speaker doesn't need to use the subject pronoun:

| | |
|---|---|
| Juan: (Yo) Soy médico. ¿Y tú? | *I am a doctor. And you?* |
| Pablo: (Yo) Soy arquitecto. | *I am an architect.* |

However, questions asked of a group require the subject pronoun when the different members of the group respond:

| | |
|---|---|
| Pepe: ¿Quién quiere café? | *Who wants coffee?* |
| Luis: **Yo** quiero, pero sólo un poco. | *I do, but just a little.* |
| Antonio: **Yo** no quiero, gracias. | *I don't, thanks.* |

When talking to the different members of a group in turns, subject pronouns can be left out when the members are addressed personally, using their names:

| | |
|---|---|
| Ana (a Luis): ¿Qué te vas a poner, **Luis**? | *What are you going to wear, Luis?* |
| Luis: Me voy a poner mi traje nuevo. | *I'm going to wear my new suit.* |
| Ana (a Paco): ¿Qué te vas a poner **tú**? | *What are you going to wear?* |

In the first question, Ana could have used **tú**, as subject pronouns can be used with proper nouns. In the second question, Ana has to use **tú**, as she is now asking the same question to another member of the group.

When asking **¿Quién es?** (*Who is it?*) at the door or on the phone, the subject pronoun is always left out. If the one who answers this question is known to the person asking, the subject pronoun must follow the verb (inversion); but if nouns are used (proper or common), the subject pronoun can be omitted:

| | |
|---|---|
| María: ¿Quién es? | *Who is it?* |
| Pedro: Soy **yo**, tu cuñado. | *It's me, your brother-in-law.* |

If the one who answers is a stranger to the person asking, the subject pronoun can be omitted and it usually is. If used, it is never inverted with the verb:

| | |
|---|---|
| María: ¿Quién es? | *Who is it?* |
| Electricista: (Yo) Soy el electricista. | *I am the electrician.* |

Questions like **¿Quién es él?** (using subject pronouns) are possible, but then the speakers are talking about somebody mentioned in the conversation or about somebody who can be seen at that moment. In pointing to someone, demonstratives are more common than subject pronouns (**¿Quién es ése?**).

In sentences of the type **Son mis padres los que**... (*It's my parents who . . .*), subject pronouns are never used. The verb must be plural if it refers to a plural subject. **Ellos son mis padres** is possible, but only if introducing them or pointing to them, although demonstratives are much more common (**Ésos/Éstos son mis padres**).

Reactions to somebody's comments require subject pronouns when the reaction refers to a different grammatical person:

| Antonio: Alguien dejó la puerta abierta. | *Somebody left the door open.* |
| Carlos: **Yo** no fui. | *It wasn't me.* |

Inversion is very frequent in such reactions, especially with third-person subjects (**Fue ella**).

There are many cases in which the speaker doesn't know who the subject is or doesn't want to mention the person responsible for an action. Sentences referring to such cases are called *impersonal sentences*. They usually consist of third-person verb forms in the plural. The subject pronoun is never used:

| Están construyendo un puente. | *They're building a bridge.* |
| Me han robado. | *They have robbed me.* |
| Me han dicho que estás enfermo. | *They've told me that you are sick.* |

In English, passive structures are often used in these cases: *A bridge is being built. I have been robbed. I've been told that you are sick.*

When Spanish speakers introduce themselves, they don't usually use subject pronouns, but when they introduce other people, they use either subject pronouns or, much more commonly, demonstratives:

| **Éste** es Pablo. | *This is Pablo.* |
| **Éstos** son mis hijos, Pedro y Ana. | *These are my children, Pedro and Ana.* |
| **Ésta** es Carla. (Ella) Es enfermera. | *This is Carla. She's a nurse.* |

In the third example, it is obvious that **enfermera** refers to Carla, so it is not necessary to use the subject pronoun.

Subject pronouns are often used to make a clear distinction between one grammatical person and another:

| **Ella** es muy amable, pero **él** no. | *She is very kind, but he isn't.* |
| **Yo** voy a hacer eso, no **tú**. | *I am going to do that, not you.* |

When the speaker needs to define/clarify exactly who the subject is, subject pronouns aren't usually omitted, especially with relative pronouns:

| **Ella** es la que rompió el jarrón. | *She is the one who broke the vase.* |
| **Yo** soy el que tiene la llave. | *I am the one who has the key.* |

Sometimes the use of third-person verb forms can be rather confusing without subject pronouns. If the context is not clear, a sentence like **Es de Brasil** can be problematic for the person spoken to, as the verb form **es** can go with different subjects (**Usted es de Brasil**, **Ella es de Brasil**, etc.). In such cases, subject pronouns are usually not omitted. In most other cases, using or not using subject pronouns depends on the speaker's personal style, emphasis, and so on.

*Fill in the blanks with the appropriate object pronouns. In a few cases, no object pronoun is required.*

1. ___*Le*___ voy a decir a Andrea que Luis no ___*la*___ va a invitar (a ella).

2. No ___*les*___ puedo decir nada a ustedes sobre esto.

3. A Miguel ___*lo*___ van a operar esta semana.

4. A Marta no ___*la*___ van a dar nada.

5. ___*Le*___ voy a comprar a mi hijo una moto para su cumpleaños.

6. ¿No viste el accidente? Yo sí ___*lo*___ vi. ¡Fue terrible!

7. Ya sé que quieres usar mi bicicleta, pero yo ___*la*___ necesito esta tarde.

8. A los hijos de Juan no ___*les*___ ha pasado nada. ___*Les*___ acabo de ver sanos y salvos por ahí.

*Underline the correct choice (the hyphen means that no object pronoun is necessary).*

1. Al perro **lo/le** tienes que dar de comer. Al pobre animal **lo/le** tienes muerto de hambre.

2. No **le/-** voy a ver a Tomás esta noche, pero a Luisa sí **le/la** voy a ver.

3. Si haces eso otra vez, ¡**te/-** juro que **te/-** mato!

4. No **le/-** tengo que llevar a mi hermano al colegio.

5. Oye, Julio, ¿**mí/me** puedes alargar ese boli? **Le/Lo** necesito para rellenar este formulario.

6. **Lo/-** voy a llamar a Daniel. *Le* **Le/Lo** tengo que preguntar si a su hermana **le/la** han enviado las notas ya.

7. Ella ~~mí~~/me preguntó a mí si yo sabía el número de Antonio de memoria, y yo ~~la~~/le respondí que no, pero que le/~~lo~~ tenía en mi agenda.

8. Marta me ha pedido el coche, pero no ~~le~~/se lo voy a poder prestar.

EJERCICIO

**1·3**

*Omit the subject pronoun where possible.*

1. MARCO     Buenos días, ~~Yo~~ soy Marco.

   FELIPE     Hola, yo soy Felipe.

2. ANA     ~~Yo~~ soy enfermera.

   PATRICIA     Yo soy secretaria.

3. ANTONIO     Alguien ha derramado leche aquí.

   PEDRO     Yo no lo he hecho.

4. POLICÍA     ¿Es usted de Los Ángeles?

   ROBERTO     No, ~~yo~~ soy de Nueva York.

EJERCICIO

**1·4**

*Introduce subject pronouns where necessary.*

1. AURORA     ¿Dónde vais a ir este fin de semana?

   LUIS     _Yo_ Voy a ir a los lagos. Quiero remar.

   FERNANDO  _Yo_ Tengo que quedarme en casa. Tengo que estudiar.

2. AMADOR     Son los ricos los que deben pagar más impuestos.

   ENRIQUE     Creo que tienes razón.

3. POLICÍA     ¿Puede _✓ usted_ enseñarme su documentación?

   PACO     No, no puedo. La tengo en el hotel.

*Find and correct any mistakes.*

1. A ese alumno van a tener que echar.
   *(le)* *(los)*

2. Mi jefe les quiere ver a ustedes en su despacho de inmediato.

3. No le quise decir a mis padres que había tenido un accidente.
   *(les)*

4. La profesora no lo me dijo en ese momento.
   *(lo)*

5. Pablo quiere que le hagas un favor.
   *(le)*

6. Nadie quiso venir conmigo.

7. Juan dice que él no puede venir, porque él tiene mucho trabajo.

8. A mis hermanos no les gusta estudiar matemáticas.
   *(les)*

*Replace the nouns with pronouns.*

EXAMPLE     Juan le dio **la carta** a **su madre**.     *Juan se la dio.*

                Ella no nos prestó **su diccionario**.     *Ella no nos lo prestó.*

1. Paco no nos va a querer instalar **la antena**.

   *Paco no nos la va a querer instalar.*

2. Yo les tuve que dar **el dinero** a **tus hermanos**.

   *Yo tuve que dárselos.*

3. No me han traído **la tele nueva** todavía.

   *No me han la traído todavía.*

4. Pepe le regaló **un ordenador** a **su novia**.

   *Pepe se lo regaló.*

5. A **tus hermanos** les vendí **los dos coches**.

   *Se los vendí.*

6. Si yo fuera tú, yo no le diría a **tu madre que fumas**.

   *Si yo fuera tú, yo no se lo diría.*

7. Juan no les tiene que devolver **los libros**.

   *Juan no se los tiene que devolver.*

8. Ana me va a traer **los periódicos** esta mañana.

   *Ana va a traérmelos esta mañana.*

*Determine in which of the following sentences the third-person object pronoun can be replaced by a similar one.*

1. A mi hermana no le gustan los hombres con barba.

2. Mi madre no los suele cocer mucho tiempo.

3. De acuerdo, les invitaré; aunque sabes que no me gusta hablar con ellos.

4. A mi cuñado le aterra viajar en avión.

5. A mi hijo le han castigado dos veces este mes en el colegio.

6. A mi hija aún no le han dado la nota del último examen.

*Make correct sentences with the following words.*

1. le/muy/Luis/cosas/no/bien/a/las/salieron

_____

2. no/a/quien/lo/Antonio/yo/se/contó/fui

_____

3. miedo/a/las/novia/de/encantan/mi/películas/le

_____

4. Ana/prestado/lo/ha/nos/no

_____

5. ¿/?/mecánico/lo/quién/al/se/encargó

_____

6. dice/gustan/mucho/no/le/Paco/que

_____


EJERCICIO
1·9

*Translate into English.*

1. Ella nos lo dio.

_____

2. Paco se lo envió a su hermano.

_____

3. Yo se lo dije a ella.

_____

4. El profesor quiere veros a las siete.

_____

5. Soy yo, Juan. Déjame entrar.

_____

6. La señora Antúnez nos hizo café.

_____

7. Carla nos estaba esperando en la sala.

_____

8. Juan estaba contándonos un chiste cuando ella le llamó.

_____

9. María estaba explicándoselo (a ellos).

_____

10. No quisieron enseñároslo.

_____

*Translate into Spanish.*

1. *They will have to talk with us first.*

_____

2. *She didn't want to come with me.*

_____

3. *Why doesn't Patricia want to work with you* (informal singular)?

_____

4. *You* (informal singular) *can give it* (**llave**) *to her.*

_____

5. *He made it for us.*

_____

6. *I have seen him in the office.*

_____

7. *I have told him that we can't go with him.*

_____

8. *She loves soccer.*

_____

9. *I will take you* (informal singular) *to your room.*

_____

10. *I can't stand Pedro!* (Use **no soportar**.)

_____

11. *I asked them if they had seen my house and they answered that they had already seen it.*

_____

12. *I need them (**gafas**) now. I can't read anything without them.*

_____

# Some/any and other determiners

## 2

Nouns like **coche** (*car*) or **manzana** (*apple*) are countable. This means that indefinite articles and numbers can be used with them:

| | |
|---|---|
| una casa | *a house* |
| dos cajas | *two boxes* |
| unos niños | *some children* |

Nouns like **aceite** (*oil*) or **agua** (*water*) are uncountable. This means that it is usually not possible to use indefinite articles or numbers with them:

| | |
|---|---|
| Hay leche en la cocina. | *There is (some) milk in the kitchen.* |
| No hay agua. | *There isn't (any) water.* |

This unit covers the different possibilities Spanish offers in translating *some* and *any* and their compound forms as well as a selection of important determiners related to quantity.

## Some/any and their compounds

In Spanish, it is not necessary to use determiners like the English words *some* or *any*, but if the speaker wants to be more precise or specific, there are several possibilities. **Algo de** and **un poco de**, which are masculine singular constructions, mean *some* or *a little* and are used with uncountable nouns (masculine and feminine) in affirmative sentences and in questions:

| | |
|---|---|
| Hay **algo de** leche en la cocina. | *There is some/a little milk in the kitchen.* |
| Hay **un poco de** dinero en ese cajón. | *There is a little money in that drawer.* |
| ¿Me puedes dar **algo de** mantequilla? | *Can you give me some butter?* |

Unos/unas, algunos/algunas, unos cuantos/unas cuantas, and unos pocos/unas pocas are plural determiners that have to agree in gender with their accompanying nouns. They can be translated as *some* or *a few*:

| | |
|---|---|
| Hay chicos en la calle. | *There are (some) boys in the street.* |
| Hay **unas cuantas** chicas con ellos. | *There are a few girls with them.* |
| Antonio me prestó **algunos** libros. | *Antonio lent me some books.* |
| Sólo **unos pocos** alumnos van a aprobar. | *Only a few students are going to pass.* |

In negative sentences, **nada de** (literally, *nothing of*) is common with uncountable nouns to mean *not any*. **Ningún/ninguna** is common with singular countable nouns:

| | |
|---|---|
| No hay **nada de** agua. | *There isn't any water.* |
| No hay chicas en mi clase. | *There aren't any girls in my class.* |
| No hay **ninguna** chica en mi clase. | *There aren't any girls in my class (not a single girl).* |

Notice that the verb is in the singular in Spanish in the above example, not in the plural as in English.

**Ningún/ninguna** is used with uncountable nouns for emphasis:

| | |
|---|---|
| No tengo **ningún** dinero. | *I don't have any money.* |

The pronoun form of **ningún** is **ninguno**. **Ninguna** is invariable:

| | |
|---|---|
| ¿Hay niños en el jardín? | *Are there (any) children in the garden?* |
| No, no hay **ninguno**. | *No, there aren't any.* |

In colloquial Spanish, speakers very often use **ni un** (or **ni uno** if a pronoun is called for) and **ni una** instead of **ningún/ninguno/ninguna**, but never with uncountable nouns:

| | |
|---|---|
| No hay **ni una** silla en la clase. | *There aren't any chairs in the class (not a single chair).* |

**Algún**, **alguna**, **algunos**, and **algunas** are indefinite quantifiers that can be used in affirmative and interrogative sentences. **Algún** and **alguna** are common with uncountable nouns; **algunos** and **algunas** can refer only to plural nouns:

| | |
|---|---|
| Todavía me queda **algún** dinero. | *I still have some money left.* |
| Hay **algunas** personas en la calle. | *There are some people in the street.* |

It is sometimes possible to use **algún** and **alguna** with countable singular nouns, but then the quantity the speaker has in mind is really small or considered to be insignificant. A sentence like **Tengo algún amigo** (*I have some friends*) conveys the idea that the number of friends the speaker has is truly small.

**Algún** is common in sentences of the type **Algún día te arrepentirás** (*One/Some day you'll be sorry*), but if the speaker refers to the past, **algún** is not possible; **un** is used instead:

| | |
|---|---|
| **Un** día llegó una carta. | *One day a letter arrived.* |

These determiners can also be used with a similar meaning to **alguien** (*somebody*), but then there is an implication that the speaker knows who he or she is referring to:

| | |
|---|---|
| **Algunas** aún creen que estoy soltero. | *Some (women) still think that I am unmarried.* |

These terms become **ningún**, **ninguno**, and **ninguna** in the negative. The plurals **ningunos** or **ningunas** don't exist.

Remember that **uno**, **alguno**, and **ninguno** lose the final **-o** when placed before a masculine singular noun. When these words function as pronouns (replacing a noun), they retain the final **-o**:

| | |
|---|---|
| Aún tengo **alguno**. | *I still have some.* |

As was indicated, **alguien** means *somebody/someone*:

| | |
|---|---|
| Hay **alguien** en el desván. | *There is somebody in the loft.* |

**Alguien** is used in affirmative questions, but **nadie** (*nobody, no one, not . . . anybody, not . . . anyone*) is used in negatives:

| | |
|---|---|
| ¿Hay **alguien** ahí? | *Is anyone there?* |
| No, no hay **nadie**. | *No, there isn't anybody.* |

As you can see, **nadie** can follow negative verb forms, but when it acts as the subject of a sentence and precedes the verbal sequence, the verb must be affirmative:

| | |
|---|---|
| No he visto a **nadie**. | *I haven't seen anybody.* |
| **Nadie** ha estado aquí. | *Nobody has been here.* |

Similarly, **algo** (*something, anything*) is used in affirmative questions, but **nada** (*nothing, not . . . anything*) is used in negatives:

| | |
|---|---|
| He visto **algo**. | *I have seen something.* |
| ¿Has comprado **algo**? | *Have you bought anything?* |
| No he hecho **nada**. | *I haven't done anything.* |
| **Nada** ha sido decidido. | *Nothing has been decided.* |

*Somewhere* translates as **algún lugar** or **algún sitio**. When location is meant, these expressions are preceded by the preposition **en**. If movement toward a point is meant, the preposition that must be used is **a**. **Hacia** (*toward*) is sometimes used, especially when attention is being paid to the movement itself:

| | |
|---|---|
| Tienen que estar en **algún sitio**. | *They must be somewhere.* |
| Vámonos a **algún sitio**. | *Let's go somewhere.* |

In the negative, **ningún lugar/sitio** is used:

| | |
|---|---|
| No están en **ningún lugar**. | *They aren't anywhere.* |
| | (*Or: They are nowhere.*) |

*Somehow* translates as **de alguna forma** or **de alguna manera**. **De ninguna forma/manera** is used in the negative:

| | |
|---|---|
| **De alguna forma** consiguieron escapar. | *Somehow they succeeded in escaping.* |

**Cualquier** is used to mean *any* in the sense of *any one*:

| | |
|---|---|
| Coge **cualquier** carta. | *Take any card.* |

**Cualquier cosa** translates as *anything*, and **cualquiera** translates as *anybody* or *anyone*:

| | |
|---|---|
| Di **cualquier cosa**. | *Say anything.* |
| **Cualquiera** podría hacer eso. | *Anybody could do that.* |

Similarly, **cualquier sitio/lugar** means *anywhere* and **de cualquier forma/manera** means *anyhow*:

| | |
|---|---|
| Vámonos a **cualquier sitio**. | *Let's go anywhere.* |
| **De cualquier forma**, ya no me gusta. | *Anyhow, I don't like it anymore.* |

Numbers are used with uncountable nouns in Spanish when the speaker refers to type or category. For example, **Hay tres aceites de oliva en esa tienda** means that there are three different types of olive oil in that shop.

Similarly, numbers can be used with uncountable nouns when talking about drinks. In such cases the speaker is referring directly to the *content* rather than to the *container*:

| | |
|---|---|
| Camarero, **tres vinos**, por favor. | *Waiter, three glasses of wine, please.* |

Words like *beer* and *coffee* function similarly in English, but in Spanish words for many types of liquid function in this way, when *cup of* or *glass of* is understood.

# Other determiners

There are some other determiners, generally referring to quantity, that need explanation or clarification: words such as *every*, which sometimes translates as **todos los** and sometimes as **cada**. Why is this and what are the grammatical implications of using one or the other? This and other important determiners will be the subject of the following part of the unit.

## All, *everything*, and *the whole*

*All* translates as **todo**. When used as an adjective, this word has to agree in gender and number with the noun or pronoun it modifies:

| | |
|---|---|
| toda la leche | *all the milk* |
| todo este dinero | *all this money* |
| todas las chicas de mi clase | *all the girls in my class* |
| todos los alumnos | *all the students* |

**Todo/Todos** is not followed by **de** to translate *all of*:

| | |
|---|---|
| todos nosotros | *all of us* |
| todos vosotros | *all of you* |
| todos ellos | *all of them* |
| todo | *all of it* |

Notice that *all of it* is normally translated simply as **todo**.

*Everything* translates as **todo** (invariable). When this word functions as a direct object, the verbal sequence is always preceded by **lo**:

| | |
|---|---|
| Lo he comprado todo. | *I have bought everything.* |

As a pronoun, **todos/todas** can refer to **nosotros/nosotras**, **vosotros/vosotras**, **ustedes**, or **ellos/ellas**. When the context is ambiguous, subject pronouns are used:

| | |
|---|---|
| Os he visto **a todos**. | *I have seen you all.* |
| Les he dicho **a todos ustedes** que vengan. | *I've told you all to come.* |
| Les he dicho **a todos ellos** que se vayan. | *I've told them all to leave.* |

When **todos** and **todas** function as direct object pronouns, the verbal sequence is preceded by **los** or **las**:

| | |
|---|---|
| **Las** he vendido **todas**. | *I have sold all of them.* |

The *whole* translates as **todo/toda**, and *the whole of* as **todo/toda** or **la totalidad de**:

todo el grupo                          *the whole group*
todo el país                           *the whole of the country*

## Every, everybody, everywhere, and each

*Every* translates as **todos los/todas las** when the speaker refers to all the members of the group as a whole, and as **cada** (which often means *each*) when the speaker considers the members of the group individually:

**Todos los** niños aprobaron el examen.      *Every child passed the exam.*
**Cada** niño tiene su propio libro.          *Every child has his or her own book.*

With time words, the plural form is much more common, but with the word **vez** (*time*) the singular form is used:

Vengo aquí **todos los días**.         *I come here every day.*
**Cada vez** que la veo...             *Every time I see her . . .*

*Everybody/everyone* usually translates as **todo el mundo**, but there are other possibilities, such as **toda la gente**, **todos**:

Vi a **todo el mundo**.                *I saw everybody.*
**Todos** lo saben.                    *Everybody knows.*

*Each* can be translated only as **cada**:

**Cada** vez que voy allí...           *Each time I go there . . .*

Note the use of **que** when a subject and a verb sequence follow.

To translate the combinations *we each*, *you each*, and so on, **cada uno/una de** + subject pronouns is used in Spanish:

**Cada uno de nosotros** tiene hijos.  *We each have children.*
**Cada una de ellas lo sabe.**         *They each know about it.*

As you can see, **cada uno/una** acts as a singular third-person subject.

*Everywhere* translates as **en/por todas partes** when location is meant, and as **a todas partes** when movement is meant:

Están **en todas partes**.             *They are everywhere.*
Fuimos **a todas partes**.             *We went everywhere.*

# Both, either, and neither

*Both* can translate as **ambos** (masculine) and **ambas** (feminine), but in colloquial use **los/las dos** is more frequent:

| | |
|---|---|
| **Los dos** ladrones fueron arrestados por la policía. | *Both thieves were arrested by the police.* |
| **Las dos** chicas tuvieron que venir. | *Both girls had to come.* |

*We both*, *you both*, and so on, translate as **los/las dos**. The verb that follows indicates which grammatical person is referred to:

| | |
|---|---|
| **Los dos tenemos** problemas. | *We both have problems.* |
| **Las dos se casaron** en mayo. | *They both got married in May.* |

**Ambos/ambas** can also be used in these examples.

In English there is a difference between *neither* and *none* or *not . . . either* and *not . . . any*, but in Spanish **ninguno/ninguna** can be used with all of these meanings; it does not matter whether there are two elements or more than two:

| | |
|---|---|
| No he reparado **ninguno** de estos autos. | *I haven't repaired either/any of these cars.* |
| **Ninguna** de estas casas está en venta. | *Neither/None of these houses is for sale.* |

When it is necessary to make it clear that the reference is to one of two elements, Spanish uses **ninguno/ninguna de los/las dos**, **ninguno/ninguna de estos/estas dos**, and so on:

| | |
|---|---|
| No conozco a **ninguna de esas dos** chicas. | *I don't know either girl.* |

*Either* meaning *one of two* translates as **uno/una de los/las dos**:

| | |
|---|---|
| **Uno de los dos** padres puede firmar. | *Either parent can sign.* |

# Much, many, and a lot of/lots of

*Much*, *many*, and *a lot of* translate as **mucho**, agreeing in gender and number with the accompanying noun:

| | |
|---|---|
| Hay **mucho** humo. | *There is a lot of smoke.* |
| No tengo **muchos** amigos. | *I don't have many friends.* |
| ¿Hay **muchas** chicas? | *Are there many girls?* |

In colloquial language, *a lot of* can be translated by **un montón de** (invariable); this expression is rarely used in negative constructions:

| | |
|---|---|
| Tengo **un montón de** amigos. | *I have a lot of friends.* |

*Lots of* can be **montones de** (invariable in gender) or the superlative form **muchísimo** (which agrees in gender and number with the noun it accompanies):

| | |
|---|---|
| Hay **muchísimas** personas. | *There are lots of people.* |

Similar rules can be applied to *plenty (of)*.

## Little, *few,* and *several*

*Little* translates as **poco/poca**, and *few* translates as **pocos/pocas**. These words can also act as pronouns:

| | |
|---|---|
| Hay **poca** leche. | *There is little milk.* |
| Tengo **pocos** libros. | *I have few books.* |
| Hay muy **poco**. | *There is very little (money, for example).* |

A *little* translates as **un poco** (invariable) and *a few* translates as **unos pocos/unas pocas** or **unos cuantos/unas cuantas**. The preposition **de** is added to **un poco** when a noun/pronoun follows:

| | |
|---|---|
| Sólo quiero **un poco de** leche. | *I only want a little milk.* |
| Hay **unos cuantos** chicos. | *There are a few boys.* |

Diminutive forms of **poco/poca/pocos/pocas** are very common:

| | |
|---|---|
| Necesito un **poquito** de ayuda. | *I need a little help.* |
| Quiero un **poquitín** de agua. | *I want a little bit of water.* |
| Tengo **poquitas** cosas. | *I have very few things.* |

Adding the preposition **de** to **unos/unas cuantos/cuantas** or **unos/unas pocos/pocas** is not possible except in the construction **unos/unas cuantos/cuantas/pocos/pocas** + **de** + determiner + noun/pronoun:

| | |
|---|---|
| **unos cuantos de** mis alumnos | *a few of my pupils* |

*Several* translates as **varios**:

| | |
|---|---|
| Tengo **varios** libros de ese autor. | *I have several books by that author.* |
| Hay **varias** chicas en la puerta. | *There are several girls at the door.* |

*Underline the correct choice. Sometimes both answers are possible.*

1. Sólo me quedan **unas/algunas** monedas.

2. Había **un montón/un montón de** cosas extrañas sobre la mesa.

3. Nadie **ha venido/no ha venido** a la manifestación.

4. Eso lo puede hacer **cualquier/cualquiera** persona.

5. Tengo **poco/poca** paciencia con estas cosas.

6. Hablé con **ambos dos/los dos** hijos de mi jefe.

7. Me levanto a las seis **todos los días/cada día**.

8. Quieren comprarnos un regalo a **todos de/todos** nosotros.

*Provide a suitable translation for the words in parentheses.*

1. Voy a contratar a _____ (*somebody*) para que me lleve la contabilidad.

2. Sólo pude leer _____ (*a few*) páginas del libro, pero me pareció bueno.

3. Las suelo ver _____ (*every*) días, pero hoy no las he visto.

4. Me pongo nervioso _____ (*every*) vez que pienso en aquello.

5. Tengo muy _____ (*little*) paciencia, así que date prisa.

6. _____ (*Anybody*) sabría qué hacer en un caso así, menos tú.

7. Hay _____ (*lots of*) libros por todas partes.

8. No he terminado _____ (*neither*) libros.

*Insert a suitable quantifier.*

1. El examen fue demasiado fácil. _____ alumnos aprobaron con buena nota.

2. Casi _____ sabe lo que te voy a contar. Es un secreto.

3. Si inviertes en esa empresa lo perderás _____.

4. Hago gimnasia _____ día después de levantarme.

5. Sólo necesito _____ sal. Es que se me ha olvidado comprar esta mañana.

6. Ese tío es muy rico. Tiene un _____ dinero.

7. No hay _____ chica en mi clase que sepa inglés.

8. Puede que haya _____ en esa habitación. He oído un ruido.

*Find and correct any mistakes.*

1. Unos cuantos de amigos míos se van a Inglaterra.

2. Uno de los dos tendrán que quedarse a vigilar.

3. Ya no quedan ningunos asientos libres.

4. Cada día viene con alguna sorpresa.

5. Esperaremos hasta que todos los aguas vuelvan a su cauce.

6. Algunos viajeros tuvieron suerte y encontraron su equipaje pronto.

7. Nadie no ha venido todavía.

8. No hemos decidido nada aún.

*Form correct sentences with the words provided.*

1. cada/registrado/rincón/hemos

_____

2. de/he/alcohol/no/nada/tomado

_____

3. ¿/?/Ana/los/vio/a/matorrales/entre/alguien

_____

4. de/despedidos/sido/mis/han/compañeros/algunos

_____

5. dueño/todo/esto/de/el/día/serás/algún

_____

6. nadie/no/desde/llamado/ayer/ha

_____

*Rewrite the following sentences so that the meaning stays unchanged. Use the words in parentheses.*

1. Hay poquísimas cervezas en el sótano. (casi)

_____

2. Unos cuantos amigos míos participaron en la manifestación. (algunos de)

_____

3. Suelo entrenar todos los días. (cada)

_____

4. O este chico o ése tendrán que limpiar el patio. (uno)

_____

5. Nadie ha solicitado ese empleo todavía. (no)

_____

6. Nada tienes que temer. (no)

_____

EJERCICIO
2·7

*Fill in the blanks with articles, object pronouns, or prepositions.*

1. _____ totalidad _____ la materia prima es transportada mañana.

2. _____ cuantos trabajadores fueron expedientados.

3. Supongo que estarán _____ algún sitio.

4. Juan _____ vio todo desde su coche.

5. Necesito _____ poquitín _____ vino para terminar esta comida.

6. Uno _____ _____ dos agentes se quedará con nosotros.

7. Vámonos _____ algún lugar donde no haya tanto ruido.

8. Ninguno _____ esos alumnos sabe la respuesta.

EJERCICIO
2·8

*Match column **A** with **B**.*

A

1. Deben de haberlo escondido

2. El coche no tiene

B

A. a casi todo el mundo.

B. sobrevivieron a la catástrofe.

3. En esta zona se recoge la basura

4. Mis padres van a la iglesia

5. Aún me quedan

6. No creo que vayamos

7. Han invitado

8. Sólo unos cuantos

C. a ninguna parte este verano.

D. algunas posibilidades.

E. nada de gasolina.

F. cada día, excepto los domingos.

G. en algún sitio.

H. todos los domingos.

**EJERCICIO**

**2·9**

*Translate into English.*

1. Esta tarde no quiero hacer nada.

   _____

2. Había muchísima gente en la tienda.

   _____

3. Quedan poquísimos osos en este bosque.

   _____

4. Suelo verles todos los días.

   _____

5. El cartero viene a las diez cada día.

   _____

6. Cada vez que les veo me pongo nervioso.

   _____

7. Se han bebido todo el vino.

   _____

8. Nadie ha estado aquí esta semana.

   _____

9. No hemos podido hacer nada.

_____

10. Hay algo extraño en esa mesa.

_____

11. Me gustaría ir a algún lugar interesante.

_____

12. No estaban en ningún sitio.

_____

*Translate into Spanish.*

1. *We can't see anything from here.*

_____

2. *There aren't many clients left.*

_____

3. *He has a lot of games in his computer.*

_____

4. *There were some problems when the strike started.*

_____

5. *I see you have no beer in your glass.*

_____

6. *Something strange is happening.*

_____

7. *Some people think that there are aliens in the government.*

_____

8. *I'm not going to invest any more money in that firm.*

_____

9. *Some day I'll be the boss.*

_____

10. *Somehow they succeeded in seeing the president.*

_____

11. *There must be somebody in there.*

_____

12. *Let's eat somewhere quiet.*

_____

# Adjectives

## 3

English adjectives usually go before nouns. Spanish adjectives are usually placed after nouns:

| | |
|---|---|
| Es un auto **caro**. | *It's an expensive car.* |

Spanish adjectives must agree in gender and number with the nouns they accompany:

| | |
|---|---|
| Él es un **chico alto**. | *He is a tall boy.* |
| Ella es una **chica** muy **guapa**. | *She is a very beautiful girl.* |

The masculine plural form of the adjective can refer to males and females or masculine and feminine nouns together. The feminine plural form can refer only to females or feminine nouns:

| | |
|---|---|
| Marta y Ana son muy **guapas**. | *Marta and Ana are very beautiful.* |
| Marta y Pedro son muy **altos**. | *Marta and Pedro are very tall.* |

Adjectives ending in a strong **í** or **ú** (with an accent) or a consonant have no specific feminine form. To form the plural, add **-es**:

| | |
|---|---|
| Él es **iraní**. | *He is an Iranian.* |
| Ellas son **iraníes**. | *They are Iranians.* |
| Tú eres el **mejor**. | *You are the best.* |
| Ellos son los **peores**. | *They are the worst.* |

Adjectives ending in **-e** have no specific feminine form either. To form the plural, add **-s**:

| | |
|---|---|
| Juan es muy **inteligente**. | *Juan is very intelligent.* |
| Elena es muy **impaciente**. | *Elena is very impatient.* |
| Ellas son muy **inteligentes**. | *They are very intelligent.* |

Adjectives of nationality or adjectives referring to a certain region ending in a consonant form an exception to these rules:

| | |
|---|---|
| Ese hombre es **inglés**. | *That man is English.* |
| Esa mujer es **inglesa**. | *That woman is English.* |
| Tengo un caballo **andaluz**. | *I have an Andalusian horse.* |
| Tengo una casa **andaluza**. | *I have an Andalusian house.* |

There are a few adjectives that can be put before nouns (as in English), but there is usually a difference in meaning when they precede a noun rather than following it. The most common such adjectives are **bueno** (*good*), **malo** (*bad*), **grande** (*big/large/great*), and **viejo** (*old*). **Grande** becomes **gran** in the singular when it precedes a noun:

| | |
|---|---|
| Antonio es un hombre **grande**. | *Antonio is a big man.* |
| Antonio es un **gran** hombre. | *Antonio is a great man.* |

The first example refers to Antonio's physical characteristics, while the second refers to his merits. Sometimes only the context can clarify the speaker's intentions. If you say **Londres es una gran ciudad**, you may be talking about London's size (*London is a big/large city*) or about London's history, museums, banks, and so on. (*London is a great city*). In talking about situations, there is usually no difference in meaning. **Un gran problema** evokes the same idea as **Un problema grande**. In both cases the speaker has "a big problem." In this type of sentence, the use of **muy** (*very*) requires that the adjective follow the noun. **Un problema muy grande** is a common construction, but **Un muy gran problema** is highly unusual.

**Malo**, which becomes **mal** before a masculine singular noun, and **bueno**, which becomes **buen** before a masculine singular noun, don't offer special problems in this respect. **Un mal tipo** (*A bad guy*) gives the same information as **Un tipo malo**. The same is true of **bueno**. **Un buen hombre** is the same as **Un hombre bueno** (*A good man*).

**Viejo**, when put before the noun, usually refers to somebody/something that has been known for a long time. If put after the noun, it refers to age:

| | |
|---|---|
| Él es un **viejo amigo**. | *He is an old friend.* |
| Ella tiene una **casa vieja**. | *She has an old house.* |

Three or more adjectives used together are separated by a comma, except the last one, which is preceded by **y** (*and*). This conjunction becomes **e** when the following word begins with an *i*:

| | |
|---|---|
| Ella es alta, hermosa e inteligente. | *She is tall, beautiful, and intelligent.* |

Adjectives like **viejo**, **joven** (*young*), and **grande** can come before the noun in combination with other adjectives that follow it:

| | |
|---|---|
| Es un **viejo** auto **azul**. | *It's an old blue car.* |
| Es una **gran** casa **andaluza**. | *It's a big Andalusian house.* |

It is not possible to make adjectival constructions like *a broad-shouldered man* in Spanish. Such constructions have to be translated by the preposition **de** (*of*) after the noun, and then a noun and an adjective together:

| | |
|---|---|
| Es una chica **de ojos azules**. | *She is a blue-eyed girl.* |

The preposition **con** (*with*) is also possible in this kind of construction, but then definite articles have to be used:

| | |
|---|---|
| una chica **con el pelo negro** | *a black-haired girl* |

In English it is possible to put two nouns together, the first one functioning as an adjective (*garden chair*, *car factory*, etc.). In Spanish, these nouns are inverted with respect to their English equivalents and the preposition **de** is inserted between them:

| | |
|---|---|
| mesa **de cocina** | *kitchen table* |
| fábrica **de autos** | *car factory* |

In the second example, **autos** is plural because the phrase refers to a factory where cars are made.

In general, constructions in which adjectival constructions precede a noun in English are translated by inverting the English order and placing **de** between the adjectives:

| | |
|---|---|
| un paseo **de diez minutos** | *a ten-minute walk* |

In fact, these constructions correspond to: noun + **de** + physical characteristic. In Spanish it is possible, and even common, to omit the noun and use the adjective and an article. **La blanca** (*the white one*) is a feminine adjective that refers to a feminine noun that has been omitted, presumably because the context makes it clear who or what the speaker is talking about. Maybe the speaker means **la camisa blanca** (*the white shirt*) but decides not to use the noun because the person addressed knows what is meant. In the English equivalent, the adjective is followed by *one/ones: the white one*.

Since nouns referring to color are masculine, they take the definite article **el**:

| | |
|---|---|
| Mi color favorito es **el rojo**. | *My favorite color is red.* |

The use of articles before adjectives is possible in English, but only when the speaker is referring to all the members of a group (*the poor, the deaf,* etc.). This is possible in Spanish too, but then the article and the adjective have to be plural:

Los ricos deben ayudar a **los pobres**.    *The rich must help the poor.*

There are many Spanish adjectives with English equivalents that end in *-ing* or *-ed*. Some of them are:

| aburrido | *boring* | aburrido | *bored* |
| divertido | *amusing* | divertido | *amused* |
| molesto | *annoying* | molesto | *annoyed* |
| sorprendente | *amazing* | sorprendido | *amazed* |
| excitante | *exciting* | excitado | *excited* |

This could be confusing, but there is a very simple explanation: English adjectives ending in *-ing* are related to Spanish adjectives that take the verb **ser**, and English adjectives ending in *-ed* are related to Spanish adjectives that take the verb **estar**:

**Estoy aburrido**, porque la fiesta **es**    *I'm bored, because the party is*
muy **aburrida**.    *very boring.*

If there is any doubt, just decide whether the adjective being used takes **ser** or **estar**. Suppose you want to translate **Ella hizo un comentario muy divertido**. As **un comentario** (*a remark*) can't be *amused*, it has to be *amusing*: *She made a very amusing remark.*

To form comparatives and superlatives in Spanish, simply put **más** before the adjective. In superlatives, **más** is always preceded by definite articles:

Él es **más rápido**.    *He is faster.*
Este auto es **el más rápido**.    *This car is the fastest.*

**Que** is used in comparisons to mean *than* or *that*:

Ella es **más alta que** tú.    *She is taller than you.*
Es la chica **más alta que** jamás he    *She's the tallest girl (that) I have*
visto.    *ever seen.*

Some Spanish adjectives have irregular forms:

| bueno | *good* | mejor | *better* | el mejor | *the best* |
| malo | *bad* | peor | *worse* | el peor | *the worst* |
| poco | *little* | menos | *less* | el menos | *the least* |
| pocos | *few* | menos | *fewer* | | |

Like all other Spanish adjectives, irregular adjectives must agree in gender and number with the nouns that accompany them:

| | |
|---|---|
| Ella es **la mejor** de su clase. | *She is the best in her class.* |
| Ellos son **los menos cualificados**. | *They are the least qualified.* |

**Poco** (*little*) becomes **pocos** (*few*) in the plural. **Menos** has no plural form.
    Translating *fewest* requires the preposition **con** or **de** instead of a definite article:

| | |
|---|---|
| el camión **con/de menos** ruedas | *the truck with the fewest wheels* |
| la casa **con/de menos** dormitorios | *the house with the fewest bedrooms* |

These constructions are like comparatives. In fact, **con menos** implies *fewer than the rest*.
    In Spanish, the Latin suffixes **-ísimo/-ísima** and **-ísimos/-ísimas** are very often added to the adjective, which then loses its last vowel:

| | |
|---|---|
| Él es **altísimo**. | *He is very, very tall.* |
| Ella es **listísima**. | *She is very, very clever.* |

These suffixes, which are actually superlative forms in Latin, imply that the subject of the sentence possesses a very high degree of a certain quality. **Esta comida está buenísima** doesn't mean that this meal is the best; it only states that this meal is very, very good. In connection with this point, the use of *most* or *highly* before an adjective is translated using the **-ísimo** suffixes or by putting **muy** before the adjective, not by using the word **más**. *He is most polite* has to be **Él es educadísimo** or **Él es muy educado**.
    **Óptimo** (*optimum, very best, couldn't be better*) is a superlative form of **bueno**:

| | |
|---|---|
| Las nuevas condiciones son **óptimas**. | *The new conditions are the very best.* |

The adjective **malo** can become **malísimo** and **pésimo** (*very very bad, couldn't be worse*):

| | |
|---|---|
| Tus resultados son **pésimos**. | *Your results are very, very bad.* |

The adjective **pobre** becomes **paupérrimo** (*extremely poor*), although many speakers say **pobrísimo**, which is not technically correct.
    The adjective **fuerte** (*strong*) changes its stem when these Latin suffixes are added:

| | |
|---|---|
| Él está **fortísimo**. (*not* fuertísimo) | *He is very, very strong.* |

In fact, these Latin forms are no longer used as true superlatives. They simply express that the quality possessed is extreme, without comparing people or things with others in a group. Compare:

| | |
|---|---|
| Eres **malo**. | *You are bad.* |
| Eres **muy malo**. | *You are very bad.* |

| Eres **malísimo**. | *You are extremely bad.* |
| Eres **pésimo**. | *You couldn't be worse.* |
| Eres **el peor** (de todos). | *You are the worst (of all).* |

Suffixes can also be added to adjectives to turn them into diminutives. These suffixes are **-ito, -ico,** and **-illo** (which agree in gender and number with the accompanying noun):

| fuerte | fuertecito/fuertecico/fuertecillo |
| altos | altitos/alticos/altillos |
| pobre | pobrecito/pobrecico/pobrecillo |

Diminutives have several functions. Sometimes they are used to express friendly or loving feelings toward a person. On other occasions, they imply that the noun qualified by the adjective possesses a quality to a certain extent, that it more or less has that quality. Diminutives can also be used to express disdain for somebody/something:

| El coche es **rapidillo**. | *The car is acceptably fast.* |
| Esa mujer es **tontita**. | *That woman is silly (in a childish way).* |
| Es mi niña **pequeñita**. | *She is my little girl (a baby or comparable to a baby in size).* |

The use of diminutives is not restricted to the field of informal language, but its frequent use in all types of sentences can sound a little childish. However, there are regions (Mexico, for instance) where diminutives are very often used.

When using suffixes, pay attention to spelling changes in order to maintain the original sound of the adjective ending. In the word **loco**, for example, the letter **c** is pronounced like the **c** in the English verb *cut*. If **-ísimo** or **-ito** is added, the letter **c** is changed to **qu** to preserve the original **c** sound: **loquísimo**.

The adjective *far* translates as **lejano**:

| Es la ciudad más **lejana**. | *It's the farthest/furthest town.* |

**Lejano** can't be used in constructions of the type *further news*. In such cases Spanish uses **más** (*more*), whose superlative form is **máximo** (*maximum*, not *further than*):

| Tendremos **más** noticias a las ocho. | *We will have further news at eight o'clock.* |
| Ésta es mi **máxima** concesión. | *This is my furthest concession.* |

The adjective *near* translates as **cercano**:

| Ése es el pueblo más **cercano**. | *That is the nearest town.* |

*Far* and *near* can be used quite freely in the comparative and superlative in English, but in the affirmative form they have a limited use. Substitutes like *remote/distant* (for *far*) and *nearby/neighboring* (for *near*) are then used. In Spanish, the adjectives **lejano** and **cercano** have no restrictions.

With words such as *bank*, *end*, *side*, *wall*, and so on it is not possible to use **lejano** or **cercano**; instead you can use constructions like **el otro** for *far* and the demonstrative **este** for *near*:

| | |
|---|---|
| la otra orilla | *the far bank* |
| esta orilla | *the near bank* |
| el otro extremo | *the far end* |
| este extremo | *the near end* |

*Far East* translates as **Extremo Oriente**, and *Far West* is **Lejano Oeste**. With **norte** (*north*) and **sur** (*south*), the adjective **extremo** (*extreme*) is normally used. *Near East* translates as **Cercano Oriente** or **Oriente Próximo**.

The comparative forms *elder* and *eldest* are translated with **mayor**:

| | |
|---|---|
| Él es mi hijo **mayor**. | *He is my elder/eldest son.* |
| Yo soy **el mayor**. | *I am the eldest.* |

*Older* can be **más viejo** (which must agree in gender and number with the noun it modifies) and **mayor** (invariable). When comparing people, **mayor** is more polite, but when talking about things, **más viejo** is more common:

| | |
|---|---|
| Mi auto es **más viejo** que el tuyo. | *My car is older than yours.* |
| Yo soy **mayor** que tú. | *I'm older than you.* |

Comparisons can also be made with **tan... como...** (*as/so . . . as . . .*):

| | |
|---|---|
| Ella es **tan alta como** tú. | *She is as tall as you.* |
| Él no es **tan listo como** Pablo. | *He isn't so clever as Pablo.* |

Parallel increase in Spanish is expressed using the construction **cuanto** + comparative + verb + comparative + verb:

| | |
|---|---|
| Cuanto más rico eres, más amigos tienes. | *The richer you are, the more friends you have.* |

In English, gradual increase or decrease is expressed by two comparatives joined by *and*. In Spanish this is achieved by **cada vez** + comparative:

| | |
|---|---|
| Estás **cada vez más guapa**. | *You are more and more beautiful.* |
| Estás **cada vez más alto**. | *You are taller and taller.* |

English constructions with adjective + *that* are usually translated into Spanish using the sequence adjective + **que** + subjunctive:

<table>
<tr><td>Es **posible que vengan**.</td><td>*It's possible that they will come.*</td></tr>
<tr><td>Es **vital que él** nos **ayude**.</td><td>*It's vital that he help us.*</td></tr>
</table>

English constructions with adjective + *for* + noun/object pronoun + infinitive become adjective + **que** + noun/subject pronoun + subjunctive in Spanish:

<table>
<tr><td>Es **importante que él se haga** miembro.</td><td>*It's important for him to become a member.*</td></tr>
<tr><td>No es **justo que ella viva** aquí.</td><td>*It's not fair for her to live here.*</td></tr>
</table>

It is possible to use a construction similar to English in some cases:

<table>
<tr><td>Es bueno para ella nadar mucho.</td><td>*It's good for her to swim a lot.*</td></tr>
<tr><td>No es conveniente para ti hacer eso.</td><td>*It's not suitable for you to do that.*</td></tr>
</table>

A sentence such as **Es importante que ella esté con nosotros** can have either of two meanings: *It is important for her* or *it is important for us*. But the sentence **Es importante para ella estar con nosotros** means that *it is important for her*, not for us (or anybody else). Despite the "double" meaning of the construction with subjunctive forms, it is preferable to use it, as there are adjectives that don't sound natural with **para** and an infinitive. A sentence like *It is strange for her to do that* must be **Es extraño que ella haga eso**. It is not correct to say **Es extraño para ella hacer eso**.

Constructions with *too* + adjective + *for* + infinitive are translated using **demasiado** + adjective + **para que** + subjunctive:

<table>
<tr><td>Este ejercicio es **demasiado difícil para que él** lo **entienda**.</td><td>*This exercise is too difficult for him to understand.*</td></tr>
</table>

As you can see, in the Spanish sentence the direct object (**lo**) is mentioned in the second clause or part. In this case, you can also use **como para que** instead of **para que**:

<table>
<tr><td>Eso es **demasiado pesado como para que ella** lo **levante**.</td><td>*That is too heavy for her to lift.*</td></tr>
</table>

Sentences of the type *It was very kind of you to help me* are translated using adjective + **por** + possessive + **parte** + infinitive:

<table>
<tr><td>Fue muy **valiente por tu parte salvar** a esa niña.</td><td>*It was very brave of you to save that girl.*</td></tr>
</table>

When a noun is present in the phrase with **por**, the construction changes to adjective + **por parte de** + noun + infinitive:

| | |
|---|---|
| Fue muy **cobarde por parte de Antonio dejar** a su mujer allí. | *It was very cowardly of Antonio to leave his wife there.* |

As in English, it is common to use infinitives after adjectives in Spanish:

| | |
|---|---|
| Es **difícil hacer** eso. | *It's difficult to do that.* |
| Fue **extraño ver**les allí. | *It was strange to see them there.* |

These sentences express opinion about the actions (e.g., **hacer**, **ver**). If the opinion refers to some other subject, this subject is mentioned first and the adjective is linked to the verb by the preposition **de**. Compare:

| | |
|---|---|
| Es fácil hacer ese ejercicio. | *It's easy to do that exercise.* |
| Es un ejercicio **fácil de hacer**. | *It's an easy exercise to do.* |

However, this construction is usually possible only with adjectives that express a degree of *difficulty*. A sentence like *That was a stupid thing to do* cannot be translated as **Ésa fue una cosa estúpida de hacer**, which is a common type of mistake. The correct translation must be **Fue estúpido hacer eso** (*It was stupid to do that*). Here are more examples of the construction with **de**:

| | |
|---|---|
| Ese camión es **fácil de conducir**. | *That truck is easy to drive.* |
| Es un texto **complicado de traducir**. | *It's a complicated text to translate.* |

When in doubt, use the construction **ser** (or other verb) + adjective + infinitive, mentioning the subject talked about at the end of the clause:

| | |
|---|---|
| **Es aburrido hacer** eso. | *It's boring to do that.* |
| **Fue** muy **inteligente quedarse** allí. | *It was very smart to stay there.* |

Verbs like *find* and *consider* can be followed by *it* + adjective + infinitive in English. Spanish has a very similar construction, but the pronoun *it* is not translated:

| | |
|---|---|
| **Consideré estúpido seguir** negociando. | *I found it stupid to go on negotiating.* |

Exclamations with adjectives always use **qué**. If a noun is mentioned, the words **tan** or **más** link it to the adjective:

| | |
|---|---|
| **¡Qué** rápido! | *How fast!* |
| **¡Qué** corredor **tan/más** rápido! | *What a fast runner!* |

When the word **forma** or **manera** is used, the Spanish infinitive is always preceded by **de**:

| | |
|---|---|
| ¡Qué **forma/manera** más tonta **de morir**! | *What a silly way to die!* |

This is also true of other types of sentences with **forma** or **manera**, not just exclamations: **Fue una manera extraña de hablar** (*It was a strange way of talking*).

The word **hora** (*time/hour*) is often followed by **de** + infinitive:

Es **hora de cenar**.                    *It's dinnertime.*
Es **hora de levantarse**.               *It's time to get up.*

When adjectives are used with the noun **hora**, it is more common to use **para**:

Es **mala hora para cenar**.             *It's a bad time to have dinner.*

But in exclamations, the preposition **de** can be used more freely:

¡Qué extraña hora **de** venir!          *What a strange time to come!*
¡Qué hora más mala **de** levantarse!    *What a bad time to get up!*

As you can see in the first example, when the adjective precedes the noun in exclamations, **tan** and **más** are not used. The sentence **¡Qué hora más extraña de venir!** is also correct; it is much less literary than the first example.

*How* + adjective translates as **lo** + adjective:

Yo no sabía **lo difícil** que era esto.  *I didn't know how difficult this was.*

**EJERCICIO**
**3·1**

*Underline the correct choice. A hyphen means that no word is needed.*

1. Ya me he probado el pantalón azul; ahora quiero probarme **marrón/el marrón**.

2. Es maravilloso ver cómo se defienden **ciegos/los ciegos** en la vida.

3. Los **marroquís/marroquíes** aprenden español con mucha facilidad.

4. Esto se está poniendo **cada vez más difícil/difícil y difícil**.

5. **Lo/Cuanto** más alto seas, **lo/-** mejor jugarás al baloncesto.

6. Es el hombre **más fortísimo/más fuerte** que he visto en mi vida.

7. Es difícil **de/-** solucionar este problema.

8. Creo que **amarillo/el amarillo** es un color que no te sienta bien.

*Give the feminine and plural forms of the following adjectives.*

| ADJECTIVE | FEMININE | PLURAL |
|-----------|----------|--------|
| 1. israelí | _____ | _____ |
| 2. andaluz | _____ | _____ |
| 3. verde | _____ | _____ |
| 4. amarillo | _____ | _____ |
| 5. japonés | _____ | _____ |
| 6. español | _____ | _____ |
| 7. exigente | _____ | _____ |
| 8. ágil | _____ | _____ |

*Find and correct any mistakes.*

1. Es demasiado barato como para que a ella le guste.

2. ¡Qué tío más fuerte!

3. Cada vez quedan bosques en el planeta.

4. Es el hombre más educado jamás he visto.

5. Es un restaurante buenísimo, pero un poco caro.

6. La francesa comida es famosa en el mundo entero.

7. Hay que ver la guapa que es esa mujer.

8. Fue estúpido por ti hacer una cosa así.

*Fill in the blanks with adjectives from the following list. Use each only once. Make any necessary changes so that they agree with the nouns they modify.*

**caro   fabuloso   último   próximo   cuidadoso   lejano   medio   listo**

1. Tienes que ser más _____ con tus juguetes.

2. La _____ vez que vengas a la ciudad, quédate unos días con nosotros.

3. Me encantan las novelas del _____ Oeste americano.

4. Hay que ver lo _____ que es este niño. Sólo tiene cuatro años de edad y sabe multiplicar.

5. La vida en el sur de España no es tan _____ como en el norte.

6. ¡La casa de Tomás es _____! ¡Tiene diez cuartos de baño!

7. Cada vez hay más problemas en Oriente _____.

8. ¡Que sea la _____ vez que coges dinero sin mi permiso!

*Make comparative or superlative sentences with the following information.*

EXAMPLE      Estos precios son muy altos. Nunca los he visto tan altos.

*Éstos son los precios más altos que he visto jamás.*

1. Antonio no es muy inteligente. Su hermana es muy inteligente.

_____

2. Juan tiene muchos suspensos. Yo no tengo tantos suspensos.

_____

3. Esta cantidad es muy alta. No estoy dispuesto a ofrecer más cantidad.

_____

4. Podrías ayudarme con esto. Sólo te pido eso.

   _____

5. Carlos tiene cualidades. Los demás candidatos tienen más cualidades.

   _____

6. La experiencia que tuve fue aterradora. Nunca tuve una experiencia parecida.

   _____

7. Jorge es muy fuerte. Sus compañeros de clase no son muy fuertes.

   _____

8. El paciente no está hoy tan mal como ayer.

   _____

EJERCICIO
3·6

*Rewrite the following sentences using the words in parentheses.*

EXAMPLES    Ese hombre no para de acumular riqueza. (cada)

        *Ese hombre es cada vez/día más rico.*

        Si estudias mucho, aprobarás con más facilidad. (cuanto)

        *Cuanto más estudies, con más facilidad aprobarás.*

1. Si te haces más alto, jugarás mejor al baloncesto. (cuanto)

   _____

2. Ya no hay tantas casas baratas en esta zona como hace unos años. (cada)

   _____

3. No lo entiendo. Invierto mucho y pierdo más. (cuanto)

   _____

4. Yo diría que estás más guapa que ayer, y ayer estabas más guapa que anteayer. (cada)

_____

5. Me esfuerzo mucho, pero mis resultados son aún peores. (cuanto)

_____

6. Lo he leído varias veces, pero ahora lo entiendo menos que antes. (cuanto)

_____

7. Los precios no paran de subir. (cada)

_____

8. Tienen muchas cosas, pero quieren aún más. (cuanto)

_____

*Join the following sentences using* **(como) para que**.

EXAMPLE    El lago es demasiado profundo. Antonio no puede llegar al fondo sin oxígeno.

*El lago es demasiado profundo (como) para que Antonio*

*pueda llegar al fondo sin oxígeno.*

1. La película tiene demasiadas escenas inconvenientes. Los niños no deben verla.

_____

2. El coche es demasiado viejo. No podemos hacer un viaje largo con él.

_____

3. Ese restaurante es demasiado caro. No debemos invitarles ahí.

_____

4. Este documento es demasiado técnico. Carla no lo podrá entender sin un abogado.

_____

5. Este curso es demasiado fácil. Tony no aprenderá lo suficiente.

_____

6. Ana es demasiado ambiciosa. No se contentará con tan poca cosa.

_____

7. Carlos está demasiado ocupado. No nos podrá atender mañana.

_____

8. Ese médico es demasiado viejo. No operará a nuestro hijo.

_____

**EJERCICIO**

**3·8**

*Add superlative (**-ísimo**) and diminutive (**-ito**) suffixes to the following adjectives.*

| ADJECTIVE | SUPERLATIVE | DIMINUTIVE |
| --- | --- | --- |
| 1. raro | _____ | _____ |
| 2. ligero | _____ | _____ |
| 3. fuerte | _____ | _____ |
| 4. lento | _____ | _____ |
| 5. exagerado | _____ | _____ |
| 6. caro | _____ | _____ |
| 7. barato | _____ | _____ |
| 8. peligroso | _____ | _____ |

*Translate into English.*

1. La película que vi anoche es buenísima.

   _____

2. Mi abuela está mucho mejor que la semana pasada.

   _____

3. Eso es demasiado peligroso para que el niño lo haga.

   _____

4. Es la peor obra de teatro que he visto jamás.

   _____

5. Mi auto no es tan rápido como el tuyo. El tuyo es rapidísimo.

   _____

6. El alquiler que pagamos por este piso es altísimo.

   _____

7. Nunca he estado en Oriente Próximo.

   _____

8. Este autobús es lentillo.

   _____

9. Es bueno levantarse temprano.

   _____

10. Es malo fumar tanto.

    _____

11. Es muy importante que ellos sepan esto.

_____

12. No es necesario que ella limpie las habitaciones.

_____

*Translate into Spanish.*

1. *It is very urgent that he come at once.*

_____

2. *This is too difficult for him to try.*

_____

3. *It's the worst book I've read in my life.*

_____

4. *Your (**vosotros**) house is much larger than ours.*

_____

5. *It is not very intelligent to do that.*

_____

6. *The exam was most difficult.*

_____

7. *The article I read in the paper this morning is very, very good.*

_____

8. *They are extremely poor.*

_____

9. *That restaurant is rather (more or less) cheap.*

_____

10. *She is a lot taller than her sister.*

_____

11. *He is not so qualified as his brother.*

_____

12. *I saw them on the far bank.*

_____

# Adverbs

## 4

This chapter covers English adverbs that end in *-ly* and that may correspond to those Spanish adverbs ending in **-mente**. It also describes English adverbs (including those with the same form as their adjectives) that can be "tricky," alongside their counterparts in Spanish.

## The ending -mente

In Spanish, adverbs can be formed from adjectives by adding the suffix **-mente** to the singular feminine form of the adjective:

| | | | |
|---|---|---|---|
| inmediata | *immediate* | inmediatamente | *immediately* |
| extremada | *extreme* | extremadamente | *extremely* |
| obvia | *obvious* | obviamente | *obviously* |
| lenta | *slow* | lentamente | *slowly* |

Adjectives that have the same form in the feminine as in the masculine take the suffix **-mente** without any changes:

| | | | |
|---|---|---|---|
| feliz | *happy* | felizmente | *happily* |
| final | *final* | finalmente | *finally* |

By adding **-mente** to an adjective it is possible to form many adverbs of manner, among others, but it is not possible with all Spanish adjectives.

English has a certain number of adjectives that end in *-ly*. They must not be confused with adverbs; they can't be translated by adding **-mente** to a Spanish adjective:

| | | | |
|---|---|---|---|
| probable | *likely* | simpático, amigable | *friendly* |
| solo, solitario | *lonely* | encantador | *lovely* |

Such English adjectives can have an adverbial function using the construction *in a . . . way*. Its counterpart in Spanish can be the constructions **de forma** + singular feminine adjective or **de modo** + singular masculine adjective, although in many cases it is possible and even common to use the suffix **-mente**:

| | |
|---|---|
| Ella me saludó **de forma amigable**. (O: Ella me saludó **amigablemente**.) | *She greeted me in a friendly way.* |
| Juan se comportó **de forma encantadora**. (O: Juan se comportó **encantadoramente**.) | *Juan behaved in a lovely way.* |
| **Es probable que** vengan. | *They are likely to come.* (Or: *It's probable that they will come.*) |
| **Probablemente** vengan. | *They will probably come.* |

The Spanish adjectives **solo** (*alone*) and **solitario** (*lonely*) mustn't be confused with the adverbs **sólo** and **solamente**, which mean *only, just*:

| | |
|---|---|
| Sólo/Solamente quiero leche. | *I only/just want some milk.* |
| ¡Me siento tan solo! | *I feel so lonely!* |

The adjective **solitario** usually refers to the fact that there are no other people/things involved. Sometimes it denotes a preference to be alone:

| | |
|---|---|
| Luis es un hombre **solitario**. | *Luis is a lonely man.* |
| Un lugar tan **solitario** me da miedo. | *Such a lonely place frightens me.* |

**Solitariamente**, **en solitario**, and **de forma solitaria** are possible adverbial constructions, although the adjective **solo** is very often used instead:

| | |
|---|---|
| Me gusta actuar **solitariamente/solo/ en solitario**. | *I like acting alone.* |
| Ella lo hizo **sola/en solitario**. | *She did it alone/by herself.* |

Some Spanish adverbs ending in **-mente** have a narrower meaning than their corresponding adjectives in English:

| | |
|---|---|
| Les hablé **fríamente**. | *I spoke to them coldly.* |
| Discutimos el tema **acaloradamente**. | *We discussed the subject hotly.* |
| El público aplaudió **calurosamente**. | *The public applauded warmly.* |

Sometimes, rather than using an adverb, a Spanish speaker uses another type of construction; for example, to say *She is warmly dressed*, a Spanish speaker would say **Ella lleva ropa de abrigo**, avoiding **calurosamente**. *Coolly*, meaning *calmly/courageously*, can be translated as **fríamente**, but **con sangre fría** is much more common. *Presently*, meaning *soon*, can't be translated as **presentemente** but as **pronto**:

| | |
|---|---|
| Llevábamos **ropa de abrigo** (o: **ropa de invierno**), porque hacía mucho frío. | *We were warmly dressed because it was very cold.* |
| El policía reaccionó **con sangre fría** y consiguió capturar a los terroristas. | *The policeman reacted coolly (under pressure) and succeeded in capturing the terrorists.* |
| Las autoridades llegarán **pronto**. | *The authorities will arrive presently.* |

Don't confuse **con sangre fría**, which means *coolly*, with **a sangre fría**, which means *in cold blood*.

# Spanish adjectives as adverbs

Some Spanish adjectives can be used as adverbs, but when this is the case, they do not end in -**mente** and are in the masculine singular form (not the feminine or plural):

| | |
|---|---|
| Fuimos allí muy **rápido/rápidamente**. | *We went there very fast.* |
| Puedes marcar **directo/directamente** desde aquí. | *You can dial direct from here.* |
| Fuimos **directo/recto/directamente** a Madrid. | *We went straight to Madrid.* |
| Estamos trabajando muy **duro/duramente**. | *We are working very hard.* |

It is important that you remember that adjectives agree in gender and number with the nouns they modify:

| | |
|---|---|
| un hombre **guapo** | *a handsome man* |
| una mujer muy **guapa** | *a very beautiful woman* |
| pueblos muy **bonitos** | *very pretty villages* |

But when adjectives are used as adverbs, only the masculine form is possible:

| | |
|---|---|
| Ella canta muy **bonito**. | *She sings very prettily.* |

If you think this is grammatically confusing, the reason for it is very simple. Adjectives refer to nouns (e.g., *the villages are very pretty*) and adverbs refer to the action represented by the verb (e.g., *her action of singing sounds very nice*).

Following are some common adjectives that are often used as adverbs.

## Fácil

The adjective **fácil** (*easy*) can sometimes act as an adverb, especially in colloquial language, instead of the adverb **fácilmente**. This most often happens when the direct object is singular and in short answers. With plural direct objects, **fácilmente** is preferable:

| | |
|---|---|
| Antonio lo hace todo muy **fácil**. | *Antonio does everything very easily.* |
| ¿Cómo los puse allí? Muy **fácil**. Con una pequeña grúa. | *How did I put them there? Very easily. With a small crane.* |

**Fácil** is not used in translating *take it easy* or *go easy*. You can use **tómatelo con calma**, **relájate**, among others, to translate *take it easy*, and **ve despacio**, **no corras**, among others, to translate *go easy*.

# Regular

The adjective **regular** (*fair, medium*) is entirely different in meaning from the adverb **regularmente** (*regularly*):

| | |
|---|---|
| Mi padre juega al tenis **regularmente**. | *My father plays tennis regularly.* |
| Mi padre juega al tenis **regular**. | *My father is not a very good tennis player.* |

# Alto and bajo

The adjectives **alto** (*high*) and **bajo** (*low*) can be used as adverbs when referring to height or level:

| | |
|---|---|
| El avión volaba muy **alto**. | *The plane was flying very high.* |
| Estábamos hablando muy **bajo**. | *We were talking very low.* |

**Altamente** (*highly*) is used only in a figurative sense and frequently before past participles:

| | |
|---|---|
| Ella es **altamente** apreciada en la empresa. | *She is highly appreciated in the firm.* |

**Bajamente** doesn't exist in such contexts; it is used only in the context of bad social behavior. **Muy abajo** (*very low*) and **muy arriba** (*very high*) are suitable alternatives, especially when referring to position/location. Both constructions are uncommon before past participles:

| | |
|---|---|
| Él está situado **muy abajo** en la empresa. | *He is situated very low in the firm.* |

When the reference is to volume, sound, and so on, the adjectives **alto** and **bajo** aren't normally used as adverbs with the verb **estar**. With other verbs they can be used as adverbs:

| | |
|---|---|
| La televisión **está** muy **alta**. | *The television is very loud.* |
| La música **está** demasiado **baja**. | *The music is too low.* |

But:

| | |
|---|---|
| No la **tires** muy **alto**. | *Don't throw it very high.* |
| Habla **bajito**. (*diminutive of* bajo) | *Speak low (in a low voice).* |

## Flojo, fuerte, igual, and suave

The adjectives **flojo** (*loose, slack*), **fuerte** (*strong*), **igual** (*equal, alike*), and **suave** (*soft*) often act as adverbs (the suffix -**mente** is very common with all of these except **flojo**):

| | |
|---|---|
| Dale **flojo**. | *Hit it softly.* |
| Empuja **fuerte**. | *Push strongly.* |
| Ellos se vistieron **igual**. | *They were dressed alike.* |
| Ella habla muy **suave**. | *She speaks very softly.* |

**Flojo** and **fuerte** can also refer to volume, sound, and so on. In that case they usually act as adjectives with the verb **estar**. With other verbs they can be used as adverbs, especially in their diminutive forms:

| | |
|---|---|
| **Puse** todas las canciones muy **fuerte**. | *I put on all the songs very loud.* |
| **Pon** la tele **bajito**. | *Put the TV on low.* |

But:

| | |
|---|---|
| Esas canciones **estaban** muy **fuertes**. | *Those songs were very loud.* |
| La música **estaba** muy **bajita**. | *The music was very low.* |

The suffix -**ito** is much more common than the suffixes -**ico** or -**illo** for diminutive forms of adjectives that function as adverbs. The suffix -**ico** is fairly common in some areas in northern Spain, and -**illo** is often used in southern Spain, but in most Latin American countries the form -**ito** is preferable:

| | |
|---|---|
| Estaban hablando **bajito**. | *They were talking low.* |

# English adjectives as adverbs

There are many English adjectives that can be used as adverbs, but they can show notable differences with regard to their Spanish counterparts.

## Back

*Back* translates as **de vuelta** or **de regreso** when it acts as an adverb:

| | |
|---|---|
| Estábamos **de vuelta** a las seis. | *We were back at six.* |

However, it is much more common to use a verb of movement:

| | |
|---|---|
| **Regresaremos** antes del lunes. | *We will be back before Monday.* |
| **Volvimos** para recoger a los niños. | *We went back to pick up the children.* |

When *back* implies movement *to the back side of a place*, it translates as **atrás**, **hacia atrás**, or **para atrás**:

Estábamos delante, pero el policía nos dijo que nos fuéramos **hacia atrás**.

*We were in (the) front, but the policeman told us to move back.*

**Atrás**, not **hacia atrás** or **para atrás**, can also refer to position/location:

Vuestras cosas están **atrás**.　　　*Your things are in (the) back.*

## Cheap

The English adjective *cheap* is often used instead of *cheaply*, but in Spanish **barato** is most often used as an adjective (agreeing in gender and number with the noun it modifies), not as an adverb:

Las compré muy **baratas**. (*not* barato)　　　*I bought them very cheap.*

When the direct object is not mentioned, **barato** can be used as an adverb:

Juan siempre compra **barato**.　　　*Juan always buys (things) cheaply.*

## Clean

In colloquial English, *clean* becomes an adverb with the verb *forget*, the prepositions *over* and *through*, and the adverbs *away* and *out*. When this is the case, *clean* has no relationship with the Spanish adjective **limpio**. Other translations are then necessary, although in many cases it is better not to translate it:

Ana no vino a mi cumpleaños. Lo olvidó **completamente/por completo**.

*Ana didn't come to my birthday party. She clean forgot.*

El tigre saltó la pared **fácilmente/sin problemas**.

*The tiger jumped clean over the wall.*

Él atravesó la pared **literalmente**.

*He went clean through the wall.*

El globo sobrevoló la montaña **completamente**.

*The balloon flew clean over the mountain.*

In the previous example, **sobrevolar** means *to fly over*.

*Clean* is not easy to translate in sentences like *The cattle got clean away*. In such cases it is much better to use the verb **conseguir** (*manage, succeed in*) followed by the verb **escapar** (*escape*). The English adverb *cleanly* can be translated by **limpiamente**, **hábilmente**, or **con precisión** in most cases:

El ladrón atravesó **limpiamente/hábilmente** la instalación de alarmas.

*The thief went cleanly through the security system.*

# Clear

The adverb *clearly* corresponds to the adverb **claramente** when the meaning is *distinctly, without confusion*, but it can be replaced by the adjective **claro** in this sense:

| | |
|---|---|
| Ella habla muy **claramente/claro**. | *She speaks very clearly.* |
| No puedo ver **claro** a esta distancia. | *I can't see clearly at this distance.* |

The expression *loud and clear* is **alto y claro** (not **claramente**). When the meaning is *obviously*, the adjective **claro** can't be used; **claramente**, **obviamente**, and **evidentemente** are common with this meaning:

| | |
|---|---|
| **Claramente/Obviamente/Evidentemente** necesitamos tomar una decisión. | *We clearly need to make a decision.* |

In English, the adverb *clear* is often used with *of* to mean *not touching*. In Spanish, this combination is usually translated using the verb **alejarse de**:

| | |
|---|---|
| **¡Aléjate de** los cables! | *Stand clear of the wires!* |

*Clear across*, meaning *right across*, is usually translated by **al otro lado de**, **al otro extremo de**:

| | |
|---|---|
| Lancé la pelota **al otro extremo del** campo. | *I threw the ball clear across the field.* |

# Close

*Close* can be translated by **cerca**, but with verbs of movement it is much better to use a verb such as **acercarse**:

| | |
|---|---|
| **Acércate**. No te puedo ver claramente. | *Come close. I can't see you clearly.* |
| **Ponte junto** a mí. | *Stand close to me.* |

In English, *closely* is used before past participles instead of *close*. In such cases, adverbs such as **estrechamente** or **íntimamente** can be used in Spanish. To mean *to be closely related (to somebody)*, in the sense of *to belong to a certain family circle*, it is much better to use the verb **emparentar**, preceded by the verb **estar**:

| | |
|---|---|
| Yo estoy **emparentado** con la familia real. | *I'm closely related to the royal family.* |
| Esto está **estrechamente** relacionado con lo que ocurrió ayer. | *This is closely related to what happened yesterday.* |

When *closely* means *carefully, with great attention*, it can be translated as **cuidadosamente**, **a fondo**, **en profundidad**, **con mucha atención**, and so on:

| | |
|---|---|
| Debes leer esto **con mucha atención** antes de firmar. | *You must read this closely before signing.* |

# Daily, weekly, and monthly

The Spanish equivalents of English adjectives such as *daily*, *weekly*, and *monthly* need the suffix -**mente** when they are used as adverbs:

| | |
|---|---|
| Esa es mi rutina **diaria**. | *That is my daily routine.* |
| Lo traen **diariamente**. | *They deliver it daily.* |
| Esa revista se publica **semanalmente**. | *That magazine is published weekly.* |
| Siempre recibimos un extracto **mensual**. | *We always receive a monthly statement.* |
| Lo recibimos **mensualmente**. | *We receive it monthly.* |

Instead of these adverbs, you can use **a diario/todos los días, cada semana/todas las semanas, cada mes/todos los meses**:

| | |
|---|---|
| Lo publicamos a diario. | *We publish it daily.* |

# Dead

The English adverb *dead* in colloquial constructions of the type *dead sure, dead certain,* and so on translates as **completamente**, **por completo**, **totalmente**, and so on:

| | |
|---|---|
| Estoy **completamente** seguro. | *I'm dead certain/sure.* |
| Él estaba **totalmente** borracho. | *He was dead drunk.* |

In other cases, other translations can be used:

| | |
|---|---|
| Estoy **agotado**. | *I'm dead tired (exhausted).* |
| Este tren es **lentísimo**. (*superlative of* lento) | *This train is dead slow.* |
| Debes ir **todo recto/todo al frente**. | *You must go dead ahead.* |

The adjective *deadly* translates as **mortal**, and the adverb *fatally* as **mortalmente**:

| | |
|---|---|
| La pobre ballena tenía una herida **mortal**. | *The poor whale had a deadly wound.* |
| El policía resultó **mortalmente** herido. | *The policeman was fatally injured.* |

# Deep

The English adverb *deeply* is used mainly to describe feelings, but its Spanish counterpart **profundamente** has a more general meaning and is used in other contexts:

| | |
|---|---|
| Estoy **profundamente** enamorado. | *I'm deeply in love.* |
| Están cavando **profundamente**. | *They are digging deep.* |

It is possible to use the adjectives **profundo** and **hondo** (both mean *deep*) as adverbs referring to physical contexts (i.e., not feelings), especially when they are preceded by the adverb **muy** (*very*):

| | |
|---|---|
| Están cavando muy **hondo/profundo**. | *They are digging very deep.* |

# Direct

The Spanish adjective **directo** can be used as an adverb with a similar meaning to the adjective *direct* in English:

Puedes ir **directo** al aeropuerto.      *You can go direct to the airport.*

The adverb **directamente** can be used instead of **directo**. While the adverb *directly* can mean *very soon*, the Spanish adverb **directamente** is not used with this meaning:

Lo terminaré **enseguida/muy pronto**.      *I will finish it directly.*

# Early

The adverb *early* translates as **temprano** when it refers to time:

Ayer me levanté muy **temprano**.      *I got up very early yesterday.*

However, it translates as **a principios de**, **al principio de**, **a comienzos de**, and so on in constructions like *early this year*. It is often translated by **pronto**, especially when the context makes it clear that it refers to an activity that has to take place sooner than expected:

Ocurrió **a principios de** este año.      *It happened early this year.*
Tendremos que recoger la fruta **pronto**      *We will have to pick the fruit early this*
    este año.      *year (right at the beginning of the*
     *season or just before the usual or most*
     *appropriate time).*

# Enough

*Enough* translates as **suficiente** when it is an adjective. It translates as **suficientemente** when it is an adverb. As an adjective, its common position is before the noun, although it is possible to place it after the noun. As an adverb, it has to be placed before the adjective:

Tenemos **suficiente** dinero.      *We have enough money.*
Pedro es **suficientemente** inteligente.      *Pedro is intelligent enough.*

**Suficientemente** can be preceded by the neuter article **lo**:

Eres **lo suficientemente** mayor.      *You are old enough.*

**Bastante** can also be used with **lo** to mean *enough*; it does not mean *fairly*, *quite*, or *rather* in this case:

Eres **lo bastante** bueno.      *You are good enough.*

## Fair

The adverb *fairly* translates as **justamente** in sentences like:

Yo no fui **justamente** tratado durante el juicio.   *I wasn't fairly treated during the trial.*

As an adverb of degree (similar to *quite* and *rather*), it translates as **bastante**:

Ella es **bastante** buena en matemáticas.   *She is fairly good at math.*

In the expressions *play fair* and *fight fair*, its common translation is **limpio**:

Veo que no estás jugando **limpio**.   *I see that you are not playing fair.*

## Far

The adverb *far* translates as **lejos**, which can only be used as an adverb of place/distance (physically and figuratively):

Ellos fueron mucho más **lejos**.   *They went much farther.*

**Lejos** can't be used as an adverb of degree. **Mucho** is common in such cases:

Él conduce **mucho** mejor que tú.   *He drives far better than you.*

The English adverbial constructions *far away*, *a long way*, and *a long way away* also translate as **lejos**. The interrogative form *how far* is **a qué distancia**:

**¿A qué distancia** vives?   *How far do you live?*

The English comparative forms *farther/further* can mean *more*. In Spanish, the word **más** has to be used with this meaning:

No tenemos **más** noticias.   *We don't have any further news.*

## Fast

You have already seen that *fast* can be an adjective and an adverb (**rápido**, **rápidamente**), but *fast* has different translations in other constructions:

Mi niño está **completamente/ profundamente** dormido.   *My child is fast asleep.*

¡Agárrate **fuerte**! ¡Vamos a saltar!   *Hold fast! We are going to jump!*

# Fatal

The use of **fatal** and **fatalmente** in Spanish is confined to contexts that talk about *fate*, *fatality*, and so on; they do not mean *deadly*. **Fatal** can also mean *very bad(ly)*, *awful(ly)*, and so on:

| | |
|---|---|
| El examen me salió **fatal**. | *I did very badly on the test.* |
| ¡Tienes unas notas **fatales**! | *You have awful/terrible grades!* |

The expression **una mujer fatal** means *a very attractive woman (who may be dangerous to get involved with)*, like **femme fatale** in French.

# Fine

The common translation for the English adverb *fine* is **bien**, but *finely* becomes **finamente**, **en rodajas muy finas/delgadas/pequeñas**, or **en trozos muy finos/delgados/pequeños** when the reference is to things that are cut into very thin or small pieces:

| | |
|---|---|
| La carne debe ser cortada **finamente/ en trozos muy delgados/finos/ pequeños**. | *The meat must be finely cut.* |

The choice of the appropriate adjective in the example above depends on how the speaker wants the meat. **Delgado** and **fino** mean *thin*, but **pequeño** means *small*.

# Free

The adverb *free (of charge)* must be translated in Spanish by **gratis**:

| | |
|---|---|
| Puedes alojarte **gratis** en ese hotel. | *You can stay free in that hotel.* |

**Gratis** (also an adjective) must be used whenever the context refers to the fact that no payment is required:

| | |
|---|---|
| Recibimos dos comidas **gratis** al día. | *We get two free meals a day.* |

In other contexts, **libre** is used to mean *free*:

| | |
|---|---|
| Jorge es un hombre **libre**. | *Jorge is a free man.* |

*Freely* is translated by **libremente**:

| | |
|---|---|
| Puedes moverte **libremente**. | *You may move freely around.* |

# Hard

*Hard* is both an adjective and an adverb in English. In Spanish, the adjective **duro** very often functions as an adverb, although **duramente** is frequently used in more formal language:

| | |
|---|---|
| ¡Dale **duro**! | *Hit it hard!* |
| He trabajado **duramente** para pagar esta casa. | *I have worked hard to pay for this house.* |

With verbs like **estudiar** (*study*) and **trabajar** (*work*), **mucho** is much more common:

| | |
|---|---|
| Estoy estudiando **mucho**. | *I'm studying very hard.* |
| Ella trabaja **mucho** en la casa. | *She works very hard at home.* |

*Hardly* has nothing to do with **duro**, **duramente**, or **mucho**. It has to be translated by **apenas** or **casi no**:

| | |
|---|---|
| **Apenas** tenemos dinero. (O: **Casi no** tenemos dinero.) | *We have hardly any money.* |

Constructions with *hardly* (*hardly ever, hardly anywhere,* etc.) are translated by **casi** followed by an adverb or adverbial construction, although **apenas** is also possible:

| | |
|---|---|
| **Casi nunca** salgo. (O: **Apenas** salgo.) | *I hardly ever go out.* |
| Ella no va **a casi ningún sitio**. | *She goes hardly anywhere.* |
| (O: Ella no va **casi a ningún sitio**. O: Ella **apenas** va **a ningún sitio**.) | |

Instead of **sitio** you can use nouns like **lugar** or **parte**.

When **casi** appears at the beginning of a sentence, the verb is not negative, but when it is introduced after the main verb, the verb must be negative:

| | |
|---|---|
| **Casi** nadie compró el libro. | *Hardly anybody bought the book.* |
| **No había casi** nadie en el teatro. | *There was hardly anybody in the theater.* |

**Apenas**, which has a similar function as **casi**, is more common before the main verb:

| | |
|---|---|
| **Apenas** había gente en la fiesta. | *There were hardly any people at the party.* |

# Ill

*Ill*, used as an adverb, translates as **mal** (*badly*). It has nothing to do with the adjective **enfermo** (*ill*). *Ill-made* is translated as **mal hecho** (**mal** is always placed before the past participle).

La casa está **mal** iluminada *The house is ill-lit.*

# Just

*Just*, when used for focusing on a specific time or place, can be translated by **justo**. **Justamente** is possible in this case, but it is falling into disuse:

Ella se cayó **justo** cuando yo llegué. *She fell down just when I arrived.*
Ellos viven **justo** enfrente de mi casa. *They live just opposite my house.*

Sometimes *just* is used with a similar meaning to *only* or *simply*. **Sólo/solamente** (*only*) and **simplemente** (*simply*) must then be used:

**Simplemente** hazlo. *Just do it.*
Yo **sólo** quería una taza de café. *I just wanted a cup of coffee.*

*Just* can mean *a short time ago* in constructions of the type *I have just been*. Such constructions are translated by the verb **acabar de** followed by infinitive forms:

**Acabo de** terminar. *I have just finished.*
Ellos **acaban de** visitarme. *They have just visited me.*
Ellos **acababan de** hacerlo. *They had just done it.*

**Hace justo** + time reference is commonly used as well:

Les he visto **hace justo** un minuto. *I saw them (just) one minute ago.*

**Justo ahora** (*just now*) is a very common expression used in all Latin American countries, but in Argentina the construction **recién** + preterit or present perfect is more common:

He estado allí **justo ahora**. *I have been there just now.*
**Recién** estuve allí. *I have just been there.*

**Recién** is in common use in all Spanish-speaking areas to refer to different kinds of actions that have just taken place and whose effects can still be seen:

recién casados *just married*
recién pintado *freshly painted*

**Justamente** is the adverb normally used to mean *in accordance with justice or the law*:

Fui **justamente** tratado por tu familia.          *I was justly treated by your family.*

## Late

The adverb *late* translates as **tarde**:

Llegamos muy **tarde**.          *We arrived very late.*

*Lately* can't be translated by **tardemente**, but by **últimamente** or **recientemente** (*recently*):

¿Has hablado con Pedro **últimamente**?          *Have you talked with Pedro lately?*

## Long

*Long*, when used as an adverb of time, translates as **mucho tiempo**. It has nothing to do with the adjective **largo** (*long [in distance]*):

¿Llevará **mucho tiempo**?          *Will it take long?*

*How long*, referring to duration, translates as **cuánto (tiempo) hace que** or **desde cuándo** if the action or situation referred to is still taking place or in effect. In other cases it translates as **cuánto tiempo**. With the verb **llevar**, only **cuánto tiempo** is possible:

| | |
|---|---|
| **¿Cuánto hace que** vives en esta casa? | *How long have you lived in this house?* |
| **¿Cuánto hace que** trabajas para él? | *How long have you been working for him?* |
| **¿Cuánto tiempo** estuviste allí? | *How long were you there?* |
| ¿Cuánto tiempo **llevas** aquí? | *How long have you been here?* |

*Too long* is **demasiado tiempo**, *so long* is **tanto tiempo**, and *long enough* can be **suficiente tiempo** or **lo suficiente** (without the word **tiempo**):

| | |
|---|---|
| Hemos esperado **demasiado tiempo**. | *We have waited too long.* |
| Esperé **tanto tiempo** que me dormí. | *I waited so long that I fell asleep.* |
| Estuvimos allí **lo suficiente**. | *We were there long enough.* |

*As long as* translates as **tanto (tiempo) como**, but when it is used to introduce a condition, it becomes **siempre que**:

| | |
|---|---|
| Viví en Londres **tanto tiempo como** ella. | *I lived in London as long as she did.* |
| Te dejaré venir **siempre que** prometas que te vas a comportar. | *I'll let you come as long as you promise that you're going to behave.* |

The comparative form *longer* referring to time must translate as **más tiempo**, and *much longer* as **mucho más tiempo**. In both cases, the word **tiempo** can be omitted:

Yo estuve allí **mucho más** (**tiempo**) que tú.     *I was there much longer than you.*

English conversational phrases such as *a long time* and *ages* can be **mucho tiempo** as well, although if the period is very long you can also say **muchísimo tiempo** or **siglos** (*centuries*):

Me llevó **muchísimo tiempo** terminar eso.     *It took me a very long time to finish that.*
Me llevó **siglos** convencerla.     *It took me ages to convince her.*

## Most

*Most* is the superlative form of *much*. Its most common translation is **más**:

La camisa blanca me gustó **más**.     *I liked the white shirt most.*

*Most* can mean *very* in formal English; in that case, it is translated as **muy**, **sumamente**, **extremadamente**, and so on:

Ella es una persona **sumamente/**
**muy** educada.     *She is a most polite person.*

*Mostly*, meaning *for the most part*, usually translates as **mayormente**, but you can also use **fundamentalmente**, **en su mayoría**, and so on:

Mis alumnos son **mayormente** ingleses.     *My students are mostly English.*

## Present

*Present*, meaning *now*, *presently*, is used in the adverbial construction *at present*, which translates as **actualmente** or as **en la actualidad**:

**En la actualidad** vivo en Nueva York.     *I live in New York at present.*

The Spanish words **actual** and **actualmente** have nothing to do with English *actual* and *actually*. **Actual** translates as *current/present*, and **actualmente** translates as *currently/ at present*. The English words *actual* and *actually* must be translated by **real** and **realmente**:

**Realmente** no estoy casado.     *Actually, I'm not married.*

*Presently*, meaning *very soon*, is **pronto** (not **presentemente**):

El tren llegará **pronto**.     *The train will arrive presently.*

## Pretty

When *pretty* functions as an adverb of degree (similar to *rather*), its translation must be **bastante**:

> Esa casa es **bastante** cara.     *That house is pretty expensive.*

In English, a distinction is made when using the adverbs of degree *fairly, quite,* and *pretty/rather*. A *pretty intelligent* man is much more intelligent than one who is *fairly intelligent*. In Spanish, the adverb **bastante** is used only when the quality possessed is present in high degree, which means that the English adverb *fairly* is not a possible equivalent in such cases.

*Prettily* corresponds to the adverbs **bellamente** and **hermosamente**, which are restricted to poetry and literary prose. In everyday Spanish, speakers use alternative constructions:

> Las señoras estaban **muy bien** vestidas.     *The ladies were dressed prettily.*
> (O: Las señoras llevaban ropa **muy bonita**.)

**Real** must always carry the suffix **-mente** when it functions as an adverb to translate *real*, meaning *really* in colloquial English:

> Ellos llegaron **realmente** tarde.     *They arrived real late.*

## Right

*Right*, when it is used as an adverb before prepositional phrases, can be translated by **justo** or **exactamente**:

> Ellos llegaron **justo** antes del almuerzo.     *They arrived right before lunch.*

When *right* means *straight ahead, all the way*, it is usually translated by **recto** or **todo recto**:

> Sigue **todo recto** hasta el primer cruce.     *Keep right on to the first junction.*

In English, both *right* and *rightly* can be used to mean *correctly*. Spanish speakers often use **bien** and **correctamente** with these meanings:

> Supuse **bien/correctamente**.     *I supposed right(ly).*
> Fueron **correctamente** alimentados.     *They were rightly fed.*

When *rightly* means *justly* (*in accordance with justice*), **justamente** is the usual adverb:

| | |
|---|---|
| Ella fue **justamente** condenada a veinte años en la cárcel. | *She was rightly condemned to twenty years in prison.* |

*Right* translates as **a la derecha** when its meaning is *to the right-hand side*. The opposite is **a la izquierda** (*to the left*):

| | |
|---|---|
| Gira **a la derecha**. | *Turn right.* |
| Gira **a la izquierda**. | *Turn left.* |

*To be right* translates as **tener razón**:

| | |
|---|---|
| Tú tienes razón. | *You are right.* |

## Sharp

*Sharp* is used as an adverb to mean *punctually*. In this case its translation is **en punto** (situated after the time) or **exactamente** (situated before or after the time):

| | |
|---|---|
| Abriremos la tienda a las nueve **en punto**. | *We will open the shop at nine o'clock sharp.* |
| Empezará a **exactamente** las siete quince. | *It will start at seven-fifteen sharp.* |

*Sharply* is often used to mean *abruptly*. Its translation then is **bruscamente**:

| | |
|---|---|
| Ella me habló **bruscamente**. | *She spoke sharply to me.* |

## Sound

Both *sound* and *soundly* are **profundamente** or **totalmente** in Spanish. Both are usually placed before the past participle:

| | |
|---|---|
| El bebé está **profundamente** dormido. | *The baby is sound asleep.* |

## Wide

As an adjective, *wide* is **ancho**, but as an adverb it has different translations, depending on the context:

| | |
|---|---|
| Yo abrí la ventana **de par en par/ completamente/totalmente**. | *I opened the window wide.* |
| Me gustaría viajar **a muchos lugares** diferentes. | *I would like to travel widely.* |

## Wrong

The adverb *wrong(ly)* is usually translated by **mal**:

Supusiste **mal** que yo era el ladrón.    *You wrongly supposed that I was the thief.*

Eso está **mal**.    *That is wrong.*

When there is a past participle in the sentence, **incorrectamente** is possible as well. **Malamente** exists, but it is falling into disuse:

Fuimos **incorrectamente/mal** informados.    *We were wrongly informed.*

*To be wrong* is translated using the verb **estar** and the adjective **equivocado**. You can also use the negative forms of the verb **tener** and the noun **razón** (*reason*):

Están equivocados. (O: No tienen razón.)    *They are wrong.*

EJERCICIO 4·1

*Fill in the blanks with the Spanish translation of the words in parentheses.*

1. Lo siento. Es demasiado _____ (*late*).

2. No te sientes ahí, porque está _____ (*freshly*) pintado.

3. Estos apartamentos son _____ (*really*) caros.

4. Ese chico es _____ (*pretty*) inteligente.

5. Nos recogen la basura _____ (*daily*).

6. No intentes girar _____ (*left*) aquí. Podría ser muy peligroso.

7. Mi hermana no sale _____ (*hardly ever*).

8. No he estado muy amable contigo _____ (*lately*). Perdóname.

9. Eres _____ (*too*) bajito para practicar el baloncesto.

10. Estudia _____ (*hard*) y te convertirás en un hombre de provecho.

*Find and correct any mistakes.*

1. El globo se encontraba muy altamente y desde él se veían las casas muy pequeñitas.

2. No te preocupes. Lo haré presentemente.

3. Fundamental como a base de verduras.

4. Hace muchísimo tiempo que no les veo por aquí.

5. Nunca repartes recto. A mí me das siempre el trozo más pequeño.

6. Los compré muy baratamente el otro día.

7. No hay que pagar. Podemos entrar libremente.

8. Os espero de espalda a las siete para cenar juntos.

9. ¿Has tenido alguna experiencia interesante últimamente?

10. Los niños son bastante ruidosos.

*Underline the correct choice.*

1. El verano va a empezar **temprano/pronto** este año.

2. Es muy **probablemente/probable** que lo traigan esta noche.

3. Abrí las puertas **anchamente/completamente**.

4. Es un experimento **extremado/sumamente** peligroso.

5. Empújalos **fuerte/fuertes**.

6. El profesor estaba hablándonos **bajito/bajamente**.

7. Son **demasiados/demasiado** buenos para nosotros. No les podremos ganar.

8. Es un chico **amigable/amigablemente**. Siempre me está sonriendo.

9. Estoy en buena forma porque entreno **regular/regularmente**.

10. **Duramente/Apenas** me queda dinero para pagar la renta.

EJERCICIO
4·4

*Fill in the blanks with adverbs from the following list. Use each only once.*

| fríamente | apenas | gratis | mal | regularmente |
|---|---|---|---|---|
| injustamente | recién | cerca | tarde | temprano |

1. Creo que podremos ver el concierto _____. Juan nos dejará entrar por la parte de atrás.

2. Los _____ casados decidieron pasar su luna de miel en el Caribe.

3. Ana fue _____ acusada de haber robado las joyas.

4. Esta carretera está muy _____ hecha. Tiene demasiados baches.

5. Luis me respondió _____.

6. Es demasiado _____ para levantarnos. Son sólo las seis.

7. Hemos llegado demasiado _____. La tienda ya ha cerrado.

8. Así no saldrás en la foto. Ponte más _____.

9. Asisto a clases de español _____.

10. _____ nos queda tiempo. Tendremos que darnos mucha prisa.

*Rewrite the following sentences using* **suficiente** *or* **suficientemente/lo bastante**.

EXAMPLES  Eres demasiado bajito para alcanzar eso.

*No eres lo bastante alto para alcanzar eso.*

(O: *No eres suficientemente alto para alcanzar eso.* )

Nos falta dinero para pagar la hipoteca.

*No tenemos suficiente dinero para pagar la hipoteca.*

1. Nos falta tiempo para poder terminar los informes.

   _____

2. No gano mucho dinero. No puedo ir a restaurantes.

   _____

3. El tiempo está demasiado mal como para ir a la playa.

   _____

4. Las maletas son demasiado pesadas. María no puede llevarlas.

   _____

5. No estudiaste mucho. Por eso suspendiste.

   _____

6. No nos han enviado mucho material. No tenemos para todos.

   _____

7. Antonio es demasiado intranquilo. No sabe lidiar con niños.

   _____

8. Elena no tiene buena preparación. No puede conseguir ese empleo.

   _____

*Rewrite the following sentences using* **acabar de** *in the present or in the imperfect.*

EXAMPLE     Ellos llegaron justo en ese momento.

      _Ellos acababan de llegar._

1. Mi madre terminó la comida en ese preciso instante.

   _____

2. Recién cogí los discos que tenías preparados.

   _____

3. Lo hemos decidido justo en este momento.

   _____

4. Juan habló con Antonio justo cuando se encontró conmigo.

   _____

5. He estado allí hace un instante.

   _____

6. Les he llamado hace un minuto.

   _____

7. Felipe me dijo en ese preciso momento que no me quedara con los libros.

   _____

8. Tomás se ha marchado hace un minuto.

   _____

*Fill in the blanks with **sólo**, which means **solamente** (only), or **solo** (alone). Remember that the latter is an adjective and agrees in gender and number with the noun it modifies.*

1. El pobre animal _____ quería jugar contigo.

2. Camarero, _____ le he pedido un café y usted me trae tres.

3. Me pongo nervioso cada vez que me veo _____ en un ascensor.

4. _____ sé que él no estaba _____ .

5. Ellas _____ querían estar _____ .

6. El café es _____ para mí; ella va a tomar limonada.

7. Mi padre me exigía _____ que estudiase los sábados.

8. A Elena no le gusta ir allí _____ .

*Some of the underlined words can act as adverbs with no changes. Others require a change or need the suffix -**mente**. Give the forms of the words that need to be changed.*

1. El policía sacó a la niña <u>rápido</u> del agua y la puso <u>suave</u> sobre el césped.

   _____

2. Los informes nos los envían <u>mensual</u>.

   _____

3. Ella me miró <u>frío</u> y me ordenó que me marchara <u>inmediato</u>.

   _____

4. Encontré las soluciones <u>fácil</u>.

   _____

5. Los veo regular sin gafas.

_____

6. Los pacientes están regular. No mejoran claro.

_____

7. Corto el césped regular. En principio, lo hago semanal.

_____

8. Es un hombre profundo convencido de sus ideas.

_____

9. Actúa tranquilo y conduce cuidadoso.

_____

10. No te preocupes. El médico estará aquí pronto.

_____

*Translate into English.*

1. Él no es lo bastante fuerte como para poder hacer eso.

_____

2. Juan se comportó con mucha sangre fría.

_____

3. Si vienen pronto, iremos a jugar al tenis.

_____

4. Todo esto es gratis. Ana me lo dio.

_____

5. Acabo de ver un accidente terrible.

_____

6. Mi secretaria es extremadamente precisa.

_____

7. Tienes razón. El restaurante está a la derecha.

_____

8. Gira a la izquierda en el semáforo.

_____

9. Sólo necesito dos horas para hacerlo.

_____

10. Pedro está altamente cualificado.

_____

*Translate into Spanish.*

1. *They are likely to arrive later.*

_____

2. *The prisoners got clean away.*

_____

3. *She is wrong. Pedro hasn't just been here.*

_____

4. *I think he did it in cold blood.*

_____

5. *The boss treated me in a very friendly way.*

_____

6. *I'll lend you my computer as long as you promise that you aren't going to play with it.*

_____

7. *Will it take you long?*

_____

8. *She hasn't visited us lately.*

_____

9. *I think that is fair enough.*

_____

10. *We'll be here at twelve o'clock sharp.*

_____

11. *There was hardly anything left.*

_____

12. *I was wearing warm clothes because it was very cold.*

_____

13. *I was dead tired after the match.*

_____

14. *The hole isn't deep enough.*

_____

15. *Study this closely. It is very, very important.* (Use **-ísimo**.)

_____

# Commands
# and requests

There are many similarities between English and Spanish in making commands and requests. This chapter covers both similarities and differences, including the cases in which it is not possible to translate English sentences literally into Spanish.

## Commands

Commands are very often expressed using imperative forms:

| | |
|---|---|
| ¡Cállate! | *Be quiet!* |
| ¡Limpiad eso! | *Clean that!* |

In the negative, the imperative is the same as the subjunctive form:

| | |
|---|---|
| ¡No toques eso! | *Don't touch that!* |
| ¡No lleguéis tarde! | *Don't be late!* |

The person addressed can be expressed by a noun preceding or following the command.

| | |
|---|---|
| No toquéis nada, **chicos**. | *Don't touch anything, boys.* |
| **Chicos**, no hagáis eso. | *Boys, don't do that.* |

The Spanish equivalent of *you* (**tú**, **usted**, etc.) is used in imperatives when the speaker wants to be rude or needs to make a distinction between people—that is, to specify the person addressed. It can precede or follow the command:

| | |
|---|---|
| ¡**Tú**, ven aquí! | *You come here!* |
| ¡Cierra la puerta, **tú**! | *You close the door!* |

An imperative like **Cierra tú** (*Close*) is slightly different from **Cierra, tú** or **Tú, cierra** (*You close*). The first is a normal imperative in Spanish. The use of the subject pronoun can express rudeness or distinguish between people (depending on the context and the tone of voice), or it can simply be an emphatic or very polite way of speaking, especially when **usted** is used. The second case (**Cierra, tú**) can only express rudeness or make a distinction. In sentences with a comma, the subject pronoun has its own stress, while in sentences without a comma, the subject pronoun has a very weak stress.

Because the verb *do* in questions and negatives has no counterpart in Spanish, the use of this verb in affirmative imperatives is not translated:

| | |
|---|---|
| Date prisa. | *Do hurry.* |
| Estudia. | *Do study.* |

Because Spanish has a different form for each grammatical person, *let's* + infinitive coincides with the first-person plural, **nosotros**:

| | |
|---|---|
| ¡Ataquemos! | *(Let's) Attack!* |
| Hagámoslo nosotros. | *Let us do it.* |

In this case, subject pronouns are used to distinguish among people. **Vayamos nosotros** (*Let us go*) implies that the speaker and the people addressed will go, excluding other people mentioned before or known by the group. In more casual conversation it is common to conjugate the present indicative of the verb **ir a** followed by the infinitive of the main verb:

| | |
|---|---|
| Comamos. (*formal*) | *Let's eat.* |
| Vamos a comer. (*informal*) | *Let's eat.* |

**Vamos a** in the example above does not translate as *Let's go*; this sentence doesn't imply movement toward a place in order to eat, just the intention of eating. More examples:

| | |
|---|---|
| Veamos. | *Let's see.* |
| Vamos a ver. | *Let's see.* |
| Hablemos. | *Let's talk.* |
| Vamos a hablar. | *Let's talk.* |

*Let's go* translates as **vamos** (informal) and as **vayamos** (formal). The form **vamos** can be confusing for English speakers. A sentence like **Vamos a trabajar** can mean *Let's work* or *Let's go to work*. If you are at a certain distance from your office or place of work, **Vamos a trabajar** implies *Let's go to work*. If you are in your office or place of work, it can only mean *Let's work*. Only the form **vayamos** implies movement (*let's go*). This means that the sentence **Vayamos a tomar unas copas** means *Let's go (out to) have a couple of drinks.*

The structure **vamos a** can't be used in the negative. If *let's not go* is meant, **no vayamos** must be used:

| | |
|---|---|
| **No** lo **hagamos** todavía. | *Let's not do it yet.* |
| **No vayamos** al cine. | *Let's not go to the movies.* |

These first-person plural forms lose the final -**s** when the pronoun **nos** is attached to them. Compare:

| | |
|---|---|
| **Llevémonos** unos paraguas. | *Let's take some umbrellas with us.* |
| **Llevémosles** al cine. | *Let's take them to the movies.* |

If **vamos a** is used, the pronouns must be attached to the infinitive:

| | |
|---|---|
| Vamos a **darles** una sorpresa. | *Let's give them a surprise.* |

The use of *let* or *have*+ noun/object pronoun + infinitive is translated by **que** + present subjunctive + noun/subject pronoun:

| | |
|---|---|
| **Que terminen** (ellos) sus deberes. | *Let/Have them finish their homework.* |
| **Que lleve** Antonio las maletas. | *Let/Have Antonio carry the suitcases.* |

Spanish subject pronouns can be omitted because the verb form clearly indicates who the subject is. It is possible to place the subject pronoun or noun before the subjunctive form:

| | |
|---|---|
| **Que Juan (él) venga** a las tres. | *Let/Have Juan come at three.* |

In English, constructions with *be to* or *must* are more common to express third-person commands than constructions with *let* or *have*. In Spanish, constructions with **que** are very common, but the verbs **deber** (*must*) and **tener que** (*have to*) are also frequently used. The verb **haber de** (*be to*) is confined to formal language, in both languages:

| | |
|---|---|
| **Deben** terminar esto antes del lunes. | *They must finish this before Monday.* |
| Ella **ha de** saber esto. | *She is to know this.* |
| Ellos **tienen que** lavar el auto. | *They must wash the car.* |

**No tener que** can be ambiguous, since it can also express lack of obligation. When in doubt, use **deber** or **haber de** in the negative:

| | |
|---|---|
| **No tienen que** saber esto. | *They aren't to/mustn't know this.* |
| **No deben** correr por los pasillos. | *They mustn't run through the halls.* |
| Ella **no ha de** leer esta carta. | *She isn't to read this letter.* |

Spanish has first-person imperative forms in the singular (**vaya yo, coma yo**, etc.). This has no practical use in everyday Spanish; these forms are restricted to the field of literature and proverbs.

As in English, it is possible to express co mmands in Spanish using the future tense:

| | |
|---|---|
| Los estudiantes **se acostarán** a las diez. | *The students will go to bed at ten.* |
| **Estudiarás** de cinco a nueve. | *You will study from five to nine.* |
| **No jugarás** con el ordenador. | *You will not play with the computer.* |

Since Spanish has no modal verbs, it is not possible to make a distinction between future sentences with *shall* and future sentences with *will*. In English, *shall* is often used in written language to state norms and rules. The future tense in Spanish can be used in both written and spoken language in expressing commands:

| | |
|---|---|
| Written: No matarás. | *You shall not kill.* |
| Spoken: Hoy no tomarás postre. | *You won't have dessert today.* |

As explained, the verbs **deber**, **tener que**, and **haber de** are often used in commands:

| | |
|---|---|
| Usted **tiene que** terminar esto mañana. | *You have to finish this tomorrow.* |
| **Tienes que** cuidar a tu hermano. | *You have to look after your brother.* |
| **Has de** limpiar esto antes de acostarte. | *You are to clean this before going to bed.* |

**Tener que** in the negative can be ambiguous, but it is often used in commands. Its meaning depends on the tone of voice:

| | |
|---|---|
| ¡**No tienes que** empujar a tu hermano! | *You mustn't push your brother!* |

The present tense of the verb **poder** (*can, be able to*) can also express a command. In these examples, it means *not allowed to*:

| | |
|---|---|
| Usted **no puede fumar** aquí. | *You can't smoke here.* |
| Ella **no puede venir** mañana. | *She can't come tomorrow.* |

Instead of **poder, estar permitido** (*be allowed to*) is very common, especially in formal language. This verb uses indirect objects, like the verb **gustar**:

| | |
|---|---|
| No **te está permitido** jugar aquí. | *You are not allowed to play here.* |

The verb **permitir** (*permit, allow*) can also express commands formally. In this case, this verb needs the reflexive pronoun **se** and the indirect object pronouns. If the subject is mentioned, it is always preceded by the preposition **a**:

| | |
|---|---|
| **A usted no se le permite** usar esto. | *You are not allowed to use this.* |

Prohibitions in English are sometimes expressed in written instructions by *may not*. In Spanish, the verbs **poder**, **permitir**, and **estar permitido** are common with this use:

| | |
|---|---|
| **A los estudiantes no les está permitido** reunirse en el vestíbulo después de las diez. | *Students may not assemble in the hall after ten o'clock.* |
| **A los estudiantes no se les permite** fumar en los dormitorios. | *Students are not allowed to smoke in the bedrooms.* |

The person expressing the command may want to sound either rude or straightforward. In that case, the verbs **querer** (*want*), **permitir**, and **consentir** (*allow*, *permit*) are often used, followed by **que** and subjunctive forms:

| | |
|---|---|
| No quiero que (usted) mencione eso. | *I don't want you to mention that.* |
| No te consiento/permito que llegues tarde. | *I don't allow you to be late.* |

The reflexive pronoun **se** is very often used in writing (notices, rules, laws, etc.) or when a speaker wants to express a command without indicating who the command comes from. It is also used to avoid mentioning the person addressed:

| | |
|---|---|
| **No se puede** aparcar aquí. | *You/One can't park here.* |
| **No se deben** usar libros en el examen. | *Books mustn't/can't be used in the exam.* |
| **No se permiten** perros. | *Dogs are not allowed.* |
| **No se permite** hablar durante el examen. | *Speaking is not allowed during the exam.* |

The grammatical number of the verb that goes with **se** depends on the noun that accompanies it. That is, the verb agrees in number (singular or plural) with the noun. Compare:

| | |
|---|---|
| No se **permite el libro** de texto. | *The textbook is not allowed.* |
| No se **permiten libros** de texto. | *Textbooks are not allowed.* |

To avoid the use of **se** twice, the second **se** + verb is replaced by an infinitive. This means that instead of saying **No se permite que se fume aquí** (which is possible, but not advisable), Spanish speakers prefer **No se permite fumar aquí**.

# Requests

A common way of expressing a request is by using the verb **poder** (*can, be able to*) in the present tense or in the conditional:

| | |
|---|---|
| ¿**Puedo** tomar más café? | *Can I have more coffee?* |
| ¿**Podría** sentarme aquí? | *Could I sit down here?* |
| ¿**Podrías** pasarme el pan? | *Could you pass me the bread?* |

There is no way of making a distinction between *may I* and *can I* in Spanish, as both are translated using a present tense. Something similar applies to the difference between *could I* and *might I*, since both forms are usually translated using the Spanish conditional. In order to sound more formal or polite, the conditional is adequate, but there are other possibilities.

The verbs **permitir** and **estar permitido** are often used in formal requests. In requests, both verbs follow the same general rules as in commands:

| | |
|---|---|
| **¿Me está permitido** usar el ordenador? | *Am I allowed to use the computer?* |
| **¿Se me permite** comer aquí? | *Am I allowed to eat here?* |

The verb **permitir** offers a much more common variation, which sounds formal and very polite; when the person making a request directly addresses the person who is going to grant the request, **permitir** does not take indirect object pronouns like the verb **gustar**:

| | |
|---|---|
| **¿Me permite** (usted) entrar? | *Will you allow me to come in?* |
| | *(Or: May I come in?)* |
| **¿Me permites** leer tu periódico? | *Will you allow me to read your paper?* |
| | *(Or: May I read your paper?)* |

The use of **se** is advisable in general requests, when the request refers not only to the person speaking but to others as well. **¿Puedo pasar?** is a request that refers only to the speaker, but **¿Se puede pasar?** can apply to anybody. **¿Me permite usted usar el teléfono?** (*Will you allow me to use the telephone?*) is a question about whether the speaker may use the phone, but **¿Se permite usar el teléfono?** is a question about a general rule.

**Dejar** (*let/allow*) is slightly more informal than **permitir**:

| | |
|---|---|
| **¿Me dejas** usar tu bolígrafo? | *Will you let me use your pen?* |

**Dejar** can be used with **usted/ustedes**, but it is unusual in requests with **se**. The verb **poder** can be used in the past (imperfect) in requests, especially when another past tense opens the request:

| | |
|---|---|
| **¿Podías** prestarme el auto esta noche? | *Could you lend me the car tonight?* |
| Me preguntaba si **podía** usar el tuyo. | *I was wondering if I could use yours.* |

The verb **gustar** can also be used to express polite requests:

| | |
|---|---|
| **Me gustaría hablar** contigo. | *I would like to talk to you. Do you have* |
| ¿Tienes tiempo ahora? | *any time now?* |

**Gustar** can be followed by **que** + (subject) + subjunctive:

**Me gustaría que** (tú) me ayudaras.            *I would like you to help me.*

**Gustar** + infinitive is a very common form of request:

**¿Le gustaría** tomar un café?            *Would you like to have a coffee?*

Instead of **gustar,** the conditional of the verb **querer** (*want*) is very often used, especially when no infinitive follows:

**¿Querrías** pasarme el pan, por favor?            *Would you pass me the bread, please?*
**Querría** ver al señor Gálvez.            *I would like to see Mr. Gálvez.*
**Querría** un café.            *I would like a coffee.*

The past tense (imperfect) of **querer** is also frequently used:

**Quería** hablar con la señora Jackson.            *I would like/I wanted to talk with Mrs. Jackson.*

**Querer** in the present is used to translate the English verb *will* in requests. The conditional of **querer** is used for *would* in a request:

**¿Quieres** sentarte, por favor?            *Will you sit down, please?*
**¿Querría** usted venir conmigo?            *Would you come with me?*

Imperative forms are also common in making requests, especially in casual conversation. Be careful that your tone of voice doesn't sound as though you are making a command. It is a good idea to add **por favor** to your "imperative" request:

**Préstame** tu periódico, **por favor**.            *Lend me your newspaper, please.*
Camarero, **por favor**, **deme** la cuenta.            *Waiter, please, give me the bill.*

The interrogative with the simple present tense is a very common and polite form of requesting something:

**¿Me pasas** la sal, por favor?            *Can you pass me the salt, please?*

This way of requesting is common when object pronouns are used. Without object pronouns, the sentence doesn't sound like a request. Compare:

**¿Me** arreglas esto?            *Can you repair this for me?*
¿Arreglas esto?            *Do you repair this?*

The verb *would* in *if you would* is translated using the imperfect subjunctive of **querer**:

| | |
|---|---|
| **Si quisiera** (usted) seguirme... | *If you would follow me . . .* |

*Would you be good/kind enough* + infinitive and *Would you be so kind as* + infinitive translate as **Sería (usted) tan amable de** + infinitive:

| | |
|---|---|
| **¿Sería usted tan amable de** dejarme entrar? | *Would you be so kind as to let me come in?* |

In these constructions, **usted** forms are not compulsory:

| | |
|---|---|
| **¿Serías tan amable de** pasarme el agua? | *Would you be so kind as to pass me the water?* |

**EJERCICIO**

**5·1**

*Make commands from the following notes, providing the missing elements. Use the clues in parentheses.*

EXAMPLES

empleados/no salir/fumar/calle (*future*)

  *Los empleados no saldrán a fumar a la calle.*

no/alimentar/animales/jaulas (se puede)

  *No se puede alimentar a los animales en las/sus jaulas.*

1. clientes/abandonar/grandes almacenes/seis en punto (tener que)

   _____

2. no/entrada/menores dieciocho años/esta discoteca (se permite)

   _____

3. chicos/no jugar/entre/flores (*imperative*)

   _____

4. limpiar/esto/antes/Pepe/enterarse (nosotros)

   _____

5. usted/no/dejar/equipaje/vestíbulo (*imperative*)

   _____

6. formularios/ser/entregar/recepción (haber de)

_____

7. no/tú/beber/alcohol/tu cumpleaños (permito)

_____

8. ellas/no/lavar/bebé (que, _imperative_)

_____

EJERCICIO
5·2

_Underline the correct choice. In some cases both answers are possible._

1. ¿Me **permites/dejas** poner el auto aquí?

2. ¿Sería usted tan amable **dejarme/de dejarme** pasar?

3. Si usted **podía/pudiera** esperar un momento.

4. Me **gusta/gustaría** que me echaras una mano.

5. ¿**Podrías/Pudieras** hacerme el favor de alargarme eso?

6. Me **apetece/apetecería** una taza de chocolate.

7. ¿**Se me permite abrir/Se permite que abra** la ventana?

8. ¿**Querrías/Quisiste** pasar a mi despacho, por favor?

EJERCICIO
5·3

_Find and correct the mistakes._

1. ¿Te apetece viniendo con nosotros?

2. No permite que los niños vayan solos.

3. Los huéspedes dejan las habitaciones libres antes de las diez.

4. ¡Callaros todos!

5. ¡Que ven aquí inmediatamente!

6. ¿Podría apartarse un momento?

7. Si la señora era tan amable de dejarme ver lo que hay en su bolso.

8. Nos reuniremos aquí todos a las seis, ¿de acuerdo?

EJERCICIO
5·4

*Translate into English.*

1. ¿Podrías mostrarme las fotos, por favor?

   _____

2. Déjame usar el tuyo, por favor.

   _____

3. Los clientes tendrán que pagar en efectivo.

   _____

4. No se permite beber alcohol.

   _____

5. Buenos días. Quería hablar con el gerente, por favor.

   _____

6. Pongámoslo detrás de la puerta.

   _____

7. Que Luisa haga el resto.

   _____

8. No hablemos de eso delante de él.

   _____

9. ¿Sería usted tan amable de sujetar la puerta, por favor?

_____

10. ¿Venden ustedes libros en español?

_____

EJERCICIO
5·5

_Translate into Spanish._

1. _Can you (**usted**) pass me the mineral water, please?_

_____

2. _Let's not sell the house yet._

_____

3. _Let Felipe buy the drinks._

_____

4. _The students will fill in the forms in pencil._

_____

5. _I was wondering if you (**tú**) were going to eat those potatoes._

_____

6. _I would like you (**usted**) to explain this to me._

_____

7. _I need you (**tú**) to give me a lift._

_____

8. _Will you (**tú**) hand me the nails, please?_

_____

9. *Don't talk so loud, boys.*

_____

10. *Allow me to open the door for you (**usted**), madam.*

_____

# Modal constructions

Once again, you will see that Spanish and English offer amazing similarities when giving advice and making suggestions. In most cases it will be possible to translate sentences literally, but in other cases you will have to know important details where translation word for word is impossible.

## Advice

English speakers often use the verbs *must, ought to,* and *should* to give advice. In Spanish, you can use the present of **deber** + infinitive for *must* and its conditional form for *ought to* and *should*:

| | |
|---|---|
| **Debes ver** esa película. | *You must see that film.* |
| Es muy buena. | *It's very good.* |
| **Deberías ponerte** un abrigo. | *You should put on a coat.* |
| **Deberías ir** al dentista. | *You ought to go to the dentist.* |

In Spanish it is common to use the verb **tener que** (*have to*) + infinitive in the present, imperfect, and conditional for advice. In the present, it is very similar to *must.* In the imperfect and conditional, it is equivalent to *ought to* and *should*:

| | |
|---|---|
| **Tienes que ir** al medico. | *You must go to the doctor.* |
| **Tenías que comer** menos. | *You should eat less.* |
| **Tendrías que tener** más cuidado. | *You ought to be more careful.* |

Some Spanish grammarians feel that the imperfect is not entirely correct in such contexts, but it is a fact that it is much more often used than the conditional form:

| | |
|---|---|
| **Tenías que ponerte** a dieta. | *You should go on a diet.* |
| **Tendrías que ponerte** a dieta. | *You should go on a diet.* |

The English construction *had better* + infinitive can be translated using the conditional of **deber** or by the construction **sería mejor que** + imperfect subjunctive:

| | |
|---|---|
| **Deberías** hablar con él. | *You'd better talk with him.* |
| **Sería mejor que hablaras** con él. | *You'd better talk with him.* |

It is possible to use the present of **ser mejor que** with present subjunctive forms. This coincides with the English construction *to be better* (*for you, him,* etc.) + infinitive:

| | |
|---|---|
| **Es mejor que te acuestes** temprano. | *It's better for you to go to bed early.* |
| **Es mejor que no discutas** con ella. | *It's better for you not to argue with her.* |

*If I were you* translates as **si yo fuera (fuese) tú/usted/vosotros/ustedes**, with a present conditional in the following clause:

| | |
|---|---|
| **Si yo fuera tú**, me **iría** andando a la oficina. | *If I were you, I'd walk to the office.* |

The first part of the sentence is often understood, which is why it can be omitted:

| | |
|---|---|
| Yo no **compraría** eso. | *I wouldn't buy that.* |
| Yo les **llamaría** ahora mismo. | *I would call them right now.* |

The verb **aconsejar que** in the present and in the conditional, followed by the subjunctive, is a direct way of giving advice:

| | |
|---|---|
| **Te aconsejo que** no fumes tanto. | *I advise you not to smoke so much.* |
| **Yo te aconsejaría que** no lo hicieras. | *I would advise you not to do it.* |

**Por qué no...** (*Why don't . . .*) + the present can be used to give advice:

| | |
|---|---|
| **¿Por qué no** lo vendes? | *Why don't you sell it?* |
| **¿Por qué no** pasáis unos días con nosotros? | *Why don't you spend a few days with us?* |

The English construction for advice *it is time* translates as **es hora de que, ya es hora de que,** and **ya va siendo hora de que**. These expressions are followed by present subjunctive forms:

| | |
|---|---|
| **Ya va siendo hora de que** dejes de fumar. | *It's time you gave up smoking.* |
| **Ya es hora de que** ordenes tu habitación. | *It's time you tidied up your room.* |

Past subjunctive forms are used when reporting:

| | |
|---|---|
| Ella me dijo que **ya iba siendo hora de que hablara** con mi jefe. | *She told me that it was time I spoke with my boss.* |

*May/might as well* can be translated using the verb **poder**. When the speaker expresses advice in a mild way (that is, the advice is not emphasized or insisted on), **por las mismas** can be added (usually preceding the verb **poder**):

| | |
|---|---|
| **Podrías** intentarlo. | *You might as well try.* |
| **Por las mismas puedes** hablar con él. | *You may as well talk with him.* |

# Suggestions

As in English, a very simple way of making suggestions in Spanish is by using the plural first-person imperative:

| | |
|---|---|
| **Demos** un paseo. | *Let's take a walk.* |
| **Visitémosles**. | *Let's visit them.* |

In everyday Spanish, it is more common to make a suggestion using the verb **ir a** + infinitive, even when no movement is implied:

| | |
|---|---|
| Tomemos un café. | *Let's have a coffee.* |
| **Vamos a tomar** un café. | *Let's have a coffee.* |

In English the question tag *shall we?* can be added to constructions with *let's*. In Spanish **¿vale?**, **¿de acuerdo?**, and so on can be added:

| | |
|---|---|
| Vamos a alquilar una película, **¿vale?** | *Let's rent a film, shall we?* |
| Vamos a tomar una copa, **¿de acuerdo?** | *Let's have a drink, shall we?* |

Constructions with *shall I/we* are translated into Spanish using the present indicative:

| | |
|---|---|
| **¿Comemos** con ellos? | *Shall we eat with them?* |
| **¿Nos alojamos** en ese hotel? | *Shall we stay at that hotel?* |

*Why don't* is translated by **por qué no** + present indicative:

| | |
|---|---|
| **¿Por qué no almorzamos** juntos? | *Why don't we have lunch together?* |
| **¿Por qué no vas** al dentista? | *Why don't you go to the dentist?* |

*What/How about* translates as **qué te/le/os/les parece si** + (subject) + present indicative. The subject of the clause with **si** is usually omitted:

| | |
|---|---|
| **¿Qué te parece si vendemos** la casa? | *How about selling the house?* |
| | (*Or: How about if we sell the house?*) |
| **¿Qué te parece si vendes** la casa? | *How about selling the house?* |
| | (*Or: How about if you sell the house?*) |

The first example refers to a speaker who wants to sell a house together with somebody, but **nosotros** is omitted. The second example is a suggestion made to one person, but **tú** is omitted.

Instead of **qué te/le/os/les parece si**, you can use **qué tal si**:

| | |
|---|---|
| **¿Qué tal si compramos** ese apartamento? | *How about buying that apartment?* |
| **¿Qué tal si hablas** con él? | *How about talking to him?* |

The imperative of the verb **suponer** (*suppose*) can also be used to make suggestions:

| | |
|---|---|
| **Supón** que les invitas. | *Suppose you invite them.* |
| **Suponga usted** que les llama. | *Suppose you phoned them.* |

In English, the verb *suppose* can be followed by past tenses (e.g., *phoned* in the example above). This is possible in Spanish too (using the imperfect subjunctive), but then the suggestion represents an idea that sounds very remote or improbable.

A very direct way of making suggestions is the use of the verbs **sugerir** (*suggest*) and **proponer** (*propose*). Both verbs are followed by subjunctive forms. If they are conjugated in the present (including the present perfect), present subjunctive forms follow:

| | |
|---|---|
| **Te sugiero que compres** esa revista. | *I suggest you buy that magazine.* |
| **Os propongo que cenéis** con nosotros. | *I propose you have dinner with us.* |

If **sugerir** and **proponer** are conjugated in a past tense or in the conditional, the imperfect subjunctive follows:

| | |
|---|---|
| Yo **sugeriría que no fumaras** aquí. | *I would suggest your not smoking here. (Or: I would suggest that you not smoke here.)* |
| **Te sugerí que fueras** a Colombia. | *I suggested your going to Colombia. (Or: I suggested that you go to Colombia.)* |

**Sugerir** and **proponer** can be followed by infinitives. When this happens, the suggestion usually includes the speaker:

| | |
|---|---|
| **Propongo discutir** esto con él. | *I propose discussing this with him.* |
| **Sugiero no ir** allí en coche. | *I suggest not going there by car.* |

In English, *suggest* and *propose* can be followed by *that* + present/past, but the word *that* may be optional. In Spanish equivalents, **que** must always be used, followed by the subjunctive:

| Ella **sugiere que** él **trabaje** para ella. | *She suggests that he work for her.* |
| **Sugiero que** usted **se quede** aquí. | *I suggest (that) you stay here.* |

Suggestions and proposals can also be made with constructions meaning *if I were you*, past subjunctive followed by the conditional:

| **Si yo fuera tú**, lo **pintaría** de verde. | *If I were you, I'd paint it green.* |
| **Si yo fuera usted**, no **firmaría** el contrato. | *If I were you, I wouldn't sign the contract.* |

**Yo que tú/usted/vosotros/ustedes** is a very common substitute for **si yo fuera tú/ usted/vosotros/ustedes**:

| **Yo que tú**, lo **haría** mañana. | *If I were you, I'd do it tomorrow.* |

# Possibility

The verb **poder** can be used to express possibility or doubt. When the context is clear, the structure of the sentence is very similar to that of the English equivalent:

| Luis **puede venir** luego. | *Luis may/might come later.* |
| Marta **puede traerlo**. | *Marta may/might bring it.* |

The conditional of **poder** expresses a more remote possibility or a higher degree of doubt:

| Antonio **podría saberlo**. | *Antonio might/could know.* |
| Mari **podría comprarlo**. | *Mari might/could buy it.* |

In referring to the recent past, the present of **poder** + **haber** + past participle is very common. The conditional of **poder** can also be used; in this case the speaker is more uncertain about the possibility:

| **Pueden haber estado** allí. | *They may have been there.* |
| **Podrían haber cogido** algo. | *They might have taken something.* |

In talking about the remote past, the speaker can use either the imperfect or the preterit of **poder**. If the speaker thinks of the action as ongoing, the imperfect of **poder** is used. In the sentence **El ladrón podía estar en la otra habitación** (*The thief may/ might have been in the other room*), the speaker emphasizes duration, the time period during which the thief may have been in the room. In the sentence **El ladrón pudo estar en la otra habitación**, the speaker considers the action as finished, so the preterit is used. This difference mostly depends on personal point of view, which means that it is very often possible to use either tense without significant differences in meaning, although the preterit is usually preferred.

Perfect forms can also be used to talk about the remote past:

| | |
|---|---|
| **Pudieron haber entrado** por la puerta de atrás. | *They might have come in through the back door.* |
| Juan **podría haber robado** el dinero. | *Juan could have stolen the money.* |

Another common construction in talking about possibility or doubt is **puede que** (invariable) + subjunctive forms. Note that the present subjunctive refers to the present or to the future:

| | |
|---|---|
| **Puede que** yo **vaya** allí. | *I may/might go there.* |
| **Puede que** ellos lo **tengan**. | *They may/might have it.* |

Past subjunctive forms usually refer to the past, but they can also be used to refer to very remote possibilities in the present or future:

| | |
|---|---|
| Puede que **estuvieran** en casa. | *They might/could be at home.* |
| Puede que **fuera** con ellos. | *I might/could go with them.* |

**Puede que** can also be followed by the present subjunctive of **haber** and a past participle. In this case, the speaker refers to the recent past or to an action that started in the past and continues up to the present:

| | |
|---|---|
| Puede que ella lo **haya enviado**. | *She may have sent it.* |
| Puede que **hayan sido** felices juntos. | *They may have been happy together.* |

**Puede que** + past perfect subjunctive usually refers to the remote past (equivalent to **puede que** + imperfect subjunctive), but it is often used to refer to an action that took place before another action mentioned in the context. It is also possible to use it to refer to a very remote possibility in the recent past:

| | |
|---|---|
| Puede que ella lo **hubiera dicho** antes. | *She might/could have said it before.* |
| Puede que **hubieran aprobado**. | *They might/could have passed (the test).* |

Instead of **puede que** you can use **puede ser que** + present subjunctive and **podría ser que** + past subjunctive. The past subjunctive indicates a higher degree of uncertainty:

| | |
|---|---|
| Puede ser que **llueva**. | *It may/might rain.* |
| Podría ser que **vinieran**. | *They might/could come.* |
| Podría ser que Juan **estuviera** enfermo. | *Juan might/could be ill.* |
| Puede ser que lo **hayan visto**. | *They may/might have seen it.* |
| Podría ser que lo **hubieran robado**. | *It might/could have been stolen.* |

Note that possibility is also conveyed using the present perfect of **poder**:

| | |
|---|---|
| Marta **ha podido estar** con ellos. | *Marta may/might have been with them.* |
| Tu hermano **ha podido hacerlo**. | *Your brother may/might have done it.* |

# Deduction, reproach, and unnecessary past actions

In the previous unit you saw the use of **deber**, **poder**, and **tener que** in commands (and that of **poder** in requests). In this section you are going to see these verbs in other contexts.

## Deduction

Both **deber** and **tener que** can be used to express deduction, what may be deduced, even in negative sentences. The verb **deber** must be followed by **de** in this case:

| | |
|---|---|
| **Debes de estar** agotado. | *You must be exhausted.* |
| **Tienen que ser** las doce. | *It must be twelve o'clock.* |
| **No debe de ser** muy tarde. | *It can't be very late.* |
| **No tienen que tener** mucha hambre. | *They can't be very hungry.* |

The present tense of **poder** in the negative can also be used, but then the speaker is more certain that the statement is true:

| | |
|---|---|
| Antonio **no puede estar** en París; le acabo de ver. | *Antonio can't be in Paris; I have just seen him.* |

Deduction referring to the recent past can be expressed by the present of **deber de/tener que** + **haber** + past participle (including **poder** in the negative):

| | |
|---|---|
| **Debes de haberlo pasado** muy mal. | *You must have had a very bad time.* |
| **Tienes que haberte sentido** horrible. | *You must have felt awful.* |
| **No puede haber sido** tan difícil. | *It can't have been so difficult.* |

**Haber** and **deber/tener** can also express deduction in the present perfect:

| | |
|---|---|
| **Ha debido de costar** mucho. | *It must have cost a lot.* |
| **Ha tenido que ser** una tortura. | *It must have been an ordeal.* |
| **No ha podido ser** tan barato. | *It can't have been so cheap.* |

Deduction about a more remote past is expressed by the imperfect or preterit of **deber/tener que** + infinitive (including **poder** in the negative):

| | |
|---|---|
| Ella **tenía que tener** unos veinte años. | *She must have been about twenty years old.* |
| **Debieron de coger** un taxi. | *They must have taken a taxi.* |
| Juan **no pudo robar** las joyas. | *Juan can't have stolen the jewels.* |

The imperfect refers to the period "around that time." The preterit refers to "that very moment."

# Reproach

In disapproving of past actions, a distinction is made between recent past and remote past. Whenever the speaker has the demonstrative **este/esta** in mind (**este mes**, **este año**, etc.), recent past is meant. To refer to the recent past, the present perfect of **deber** can be used:

| | |
|---|---|
| **Has debido hacerlo** antes. | *You should have done it before.* |

The verb **tener que** can also be used with this meaning:

| | |
|---|---|
| **Has tenido que hacerlo** antes. | *You should have done it before.* |

The preterit forms of **deber** and **tener que** are very often used to make suggestions (*should have*) that refer to both the recent and remote past (even in the Spanish spoken in Spain):

| | |
|---|---|
| **Debiste coger** el tren. | *You should have taken the train.* |
| **Tuviste que coger** el tren. | *You should have taken the train.* |

The imperfect of **tener que** + **haber** + past participle is a general construction that can express *should have* in both the recent and remote past:

| | |
|---|---|
| **Tenías que haber hecho** el examen. | *You should have taken the exam.* |
| **No tenías que haber comido** tanto. | *You shouldn't have eaten so much.* |

The conditional of **deber** + **haber** + past participle can also be used in this sense:

| | |
|---|---|
| **Deberías haber bebido** menos. | *You should have drunk less.* |
| **No deberías haber dicho** nada. | *You shouldn't have said anything.* |

The conditional of **tener que** can also be used for *should have*, but it is less frequent:

| | |
|---|---|
| **Tendrías que haber estudiado** más. | *You should have studied harder.* |

# Unnecessary past actions

Unnecessary past actions are usually expressed using the imperfect of **no tener que/no tener por qué** + **haber** + past participle:

| | |
|---|---|
| **No tenía que haber comprado** azúcar. | *I needn't have bought any sugar.* |

Still using the imperfect, it is also possible to avoid the verb **haber** when the context makes it clear that the action took place but was unnecessary:

| | |
|---|---|
| **No tenías que** ayudar. | *You needn't have helped.* |

The imperfect of **ser necesario que** and **hacer falta que** (both followed by the imperfect subjunctive) can express the same idea:

No era necesario que lo limpiaras.     *You needn't have cleaned it.*
No hacía falta que lavaras las cortinas.     *You needn't have washed the curtains.*

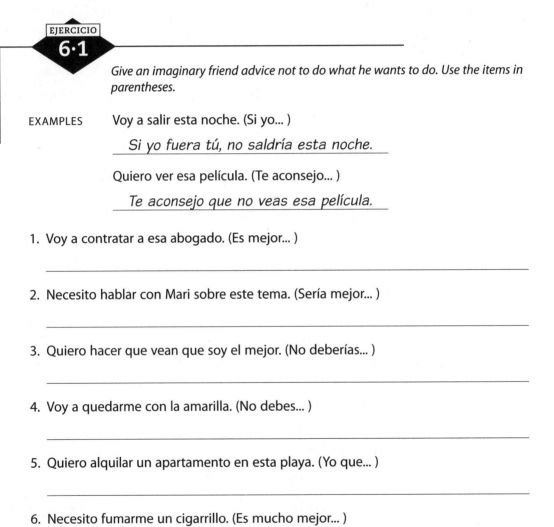

EJERCICIO
6·1

*Give an imaginary friend advice not to do what he wants to do. Use the items in parentheses.*

EXAMPLES          Voy a salir esta noche. (Si yo... )

  *Si yo fuera tú, no saldría esta noche.*

  Quiero ver esa película. (Te aconsejo... )

  *Te aconsejo que no veas esa película.*

1. Voy a contratar a esa abogado. (Es mejor... )

   _____

2. Necesito hablar con Mari sobre este tema. (Sería mejor... )

   _____

3. Quiero hacer que vean que soy el mejor. (No deberías... )

   _____

4. Voy a quedarme con la amarilla. (No debes... )

   _____

5. Quiero alquilar un apartamento en esta playa. (Yo que... )

   _____

6. Necesito fumarme un cigarrillo. (Es mucho mejor... )

   _____

7. Voy a intentar escalar esa montaña. (Sería mejor... )

_____

8. Quiero casarme con ella. (Te aconsejo... )

_____

*Underline the correct choice.*

1. **Debía/Debía de** haber más de mil personas.

2. No **hacía/hizo** falta que nos echaras una mano, pero gracias de todos modos.

3. No **tenías/tuviste** que haber hecho ese fuego en mitad del bosque.

4. No **puede haber sido/podía ser** lunes cuando ellos regresaron.

5. Puede ser que **lleguen/llegan** más tarde.

6. **Deberías/Debiste** haber dado de comer a los animales.

7. Puede que ella **haya estado/estuviera** aquí la semana pasada.

8. **Tenía que/Tuvo que** hacer mucho frío, a juzgar por la ropa que llevaban.

*Find and correct any mistakes.*

1. Ya va siendo hora de que arreglaras la moto.

2. Les sugiero que deberían intentar coger ese avión.

3. Propongo organizar una gran fiesta en el jardín de atrás.

4. ¿Por qué no preparamos unas ensaladas?

5. ¿Y si hacemos una barbacoa?

6. Leámonos las instrucciones antes de manejar la máquina.

7. Si yo fuera tú, me iría con él.

8. ¿Qué tal nos acostamos temprano?

EJERCICIO
6·4

*Translate into English.*

1. Sugiero que te pongas la otra corbata.

   _____

2. ¿Qué os parece si alquilamos una barca?

   _____

3. Debían de estar muy cansados. Por eso se fueron a la cama tan temprano.

   _____

4. No debiste preparar tanta comida.

   _____

5. Si yo fuera tú, elegiría el amarillo.

   _____

6. Hablemos con Juan antes de tomar extrañas decisiones.

   _____

7. Debiste bajarte en la otra estación.

   _____

8. Tenías que haber desayunado; ahora no tendrías tanta hambre.

   _____

9. No hacía falta que vinieras, pero gracias.

   _____

10. Creo que debería usted hacer que se lo miren.

   _____

*Translate into Spanish.*

1. *You (**usted**) needn't have helped Andrea.*

   _____

2. *I suggest your (**tú**) trying the car first.*

   _____

3. *If I were you (**vosotros**), I wouldn't stay in that hotel.*

   _____

4. *You'd better (**usted**) not read this type of book.*

   _____

5. *You (**tú**) ought to save more money if you want to buy a house.*

   _____

6. *You (**tú**) must have heard the news.*

   _____

7. *What about paying them a visit?*

   _____

8. *Let's set the table, shall we?*

   _____

9. *I would suggest ordering lamb.*

_____

10. *I advise you (**usted**) to drink less.*

_____

11. *Why don't you (**tú**) wear the dress I bought you last week?*

_____

12. *Shall we tell them to come with us?*

_____

# Impersonal sentences and the passive

It is not always possible to mention the subject of a sentence. Sometimes it is even desirable not to. If a friend of mine tells me something and I don't want another person to know that my friend told me, I must avoid mentioning him or her. If somebody steals my wallet and I report it to the police, I can't say *he, she,* or *they* if I don't know who the subject is. In these cases, we usually use impersonal sentences. In English, this problem is solved by using passive structures (*I was robbed!*). In Spanish, the passive is possible, and even common, but there are several other ways to address the situation.

## Impersonal sentences

Impersonal sentences are those in which the speaker does not mention the subject of the main verb. Here are various ways to make impersonal sentences in Spanish.

### Third-person plural verb forms

Impersonal sentences can be formed using a *third-person plural* verb without mentioning the subject:

| | |
|---|---|
| Me **han dicho** que... | *I have been told that . . .* |
| **Dicen** que... | *They say that . . .* |

In such sentences, the subject can be anybody. Very often the speaker doesn't even know who the subject is. In other cases, the speaker doesn't want to mention the subject or thinks it is understood because the context is clear:

| | |
|---|---|
| Me **van** a invitar a una fiesta. | *I'm going to be invited to a party.* |
| Nos **están llamando**. | *We are being called.* |

| | |
|---|---|
| Les **han arrestado**. | *They have been arrested.* |
| Me **han enviado** esta carta. | *I have been sent this letter.* |

To make impersonal sentences, Spanish attributes the action to a hypothetical plural subject that is always omitted, whereas in English passive structures are commonly used.

## Third-person singular verb forms

Spanish verbs whose actions can't be attributed to a person, an animal, or a thing are impersonal. These verbs are always conjugated in their *third-person singular* form:

| | |
|---|---|
| Llueve. | *It's raining.* |
| No hace viento. | *It isn't windy.* |
| Hace mucho calor. | *It's very hot.* |

Many "personal" verbs can become impersonal when they are used with the relative pronoun **que** to introduce an opinion or a comment:

| | |
|---|---|
| **Parece que** ella no sabe nada. | *It seems that she doesn't know anything.* |
| **Es obvio que** él no es el dueño. | *It's obvious that he isn't the owner.* |

As you can see, when the neuter pronoun *it* is used with no reference to a person, an animal, or a thing, an impersonal verb is used in Spanish:

| | |
|---|---|
| Está oscureciendo. | *It's getting dark.* |

## The impersonal se

Another way to make impersonal sentences is by using the reflexive pronoun **se** with the verb. The grammatical number of the verb (singular or plural) used with **se** depends on whether the object is singular or plural:

| | |
|---|---|
| Se está construyendo un puente. | *A bridge is being built.* |
| Se están construyendo dos puentes. | *Two bridges are being built.* |

When object pronouns are used after the reflexive pronoun **se**, the verb is always singular as long as there is no reference to plural nouns:

| | |
|---|---|
| Se les **ha invitado**. | *They have been invited.* |
| Se os **ha dicho** que... | *You have been told that . . .* |

If there is a reference to a plural noun, the verb is plural:

| | |
|---|---|
| Se les **han dado** las entradas. | *They have been given the tickets.* |

When the object is a noun (including a person), object pronouns are used along with the nouns, especially with the verbs **decir, ordenar, sugerir, pedir, aconsejar, advertir,** among others:

| | |
|---|---|
| Se **le** ha dicho **a Juan** que venga. | *Juan has been told to come.* |
| Se **les** ha pedido **a tus hermanos** que ayuden. | *Your brothers have been asked to help.* |

# The passive

The passive in Spanish is formed in a similar way as in English:

| | |
|---|---|
| La cocina **ha sido pintada**. | *The kitchen has been painted.* |
| Ellos van a **ser llamados**. | *They are going to be called.* |
| La bici **fue robada**. | *The bike was stolen.* |
| Eso tendrá que **ser traducido**. | *That will have to be translated.* |

The past participle used as an adjective has to agree in gender and number with the subject. Another difference from the English construction is that in Spanish an indirect object cannot be the subject of a passive sentence. The subject in a Spanish passive sentence must always be the direct object of the active sentence. A construction like **Ella ha sido dada las llaves** (literally, *She has been given the keys*) isn't good Spanish, as **ella** is the indirect object in the active sentence **Le han dado las llaves (a ella)**. Correct options are **Las llaves le han sido dadas (a ella)** (*The keys have been given to her*) or **Le han dado las llaves (a ella)** (*They have given her the keys*), which is an impersonal sentence with a hypothetical *they* as a subject. Here is another example:

| | |
|---|---|
| Me **han enviado** una carta. | *They've sent me a letter.* |

In the sentence above, which is an active, not a passive construction, **me** is the indirect object, and **una carta** is the direct object. In good Spanish, only **Una carta me ha sido enviada** is a correct passive structure, as indirect objects cannot be subjects of Spanish passive sentences.

The following steps are used to make correct passive sentences from active sentences in Spanish:

- Use only the direct object as a subject.

    Los profesores van a cancelar **los exámenes**.

- Copy the verb sequence except the last verb and leave a space between the last verb of the active sentence and the preceding one.

    Los exámenes **van** a _____.

Make sure that the first verb of the passive sentence always agrees in number with the subject chosen.

- ◆ Change the last verb of the active sentence into a past participle and place it after the space.

  Los exámenes van a _____ **cancelados**.

- ◆ Fill in the blank with the verb **ser** in the same form or tense as the last verb of the active sentence (in this case, an infinitive).

  Los exámenes van a **ser** cancelados.

- ◆ The "agent" of the active sentence can be mentioned at the end of the sentence, although it is often advisable to put it right after the verb sequence. If mentioned, it must be preceded by the preposition **por** (*by*) or **con** (*with*). Differences in usage between these two prepositions in passive sentences are the same as in their English equivalents.

  Los exámenes van a ser cancelados        *The exams are going to be canceled by*
      por los profesores.        *the teachers.*

- ◆ If there are indirect object pronouns, don't change them. Place them in the same position as they are in the active sentence.
- ◆ Direct object pronouns are turned into subject pronouns.

With these simple rules in mind, let's put the sentence **Le acaban de traer a Juan un piano** (*They just delivered a piano to Juan*) into the passive voice:

Un piano: Direct object of the active sentence.
**le**: Indirect object pronouns remain unchanged and in the same position.
**acaba de**: The first verb must be singular to agree in number with **piano**.
**ser**: The infinitive is chosen because the last verb of the active sentence is an infinitive.
**traído**: The last verb of the active sentence must always become a past participle, agreeing in gender and number with the subject chosen.

The indirect object phrase **a Juan** can be in several positions in the passive sentence, but it is advisable to put it in the same place as it was in the active sentence.

The final result has to be **Un piano le acaba de ser traído a Juan** (*A piano was just delivered to Juan*).

In English passive sentences in the *present progressive* form, the verb *to be* can appear twice. In the Spanish equivalent, the first verb is **estar** and the second is **ser**.

| | |
|---|---|
| El ladrón **está siendo** interrogado por la policía. | *The thief **is being** interrogated by the police.* |

The English construction *to have something done*, as in *I am having the house painted*, has no equivalent model in Spanish. Impersonal constructions can be used instead, as can active sentences with the person who "has something done" as the subject:

| | |
|---|---|
| Me **están construyendo** una casa. | *I'm having a house built.* |
| **Estoy construyendo** una casa. | *I'm having a house built.* |

Therefore, a sentence such as **Juan está pintando la cochera** can mean that Juan is painting the garage himself or that he is having it painted. If the context is clear, the listener will easily understand whether or not Juan is the one who is painting the garage. More examples:

| | |
|---|---|
| Me **están arreglando** el coche. | *I'm having my car repaired.* |
| **Estoy arreglando** el coche. | *I'm having my car repaired.* |
| Me **van a instalar** una antena. | *I'm going to have an antenna installed.* |
| **Voy a instalar** una antena. | *I'm going to have an antenna installed.* |

English passives of the type *He is said to be rich* are not possible in Spanish. Constructions with the reflexive pronoun **se** are used instead:

| | |
|---|---|
| **Se dice** que él es rico. | *It is said that he is rich.* |
| **Se sabe** que ella es inocente. | *It is known that she is innocent.* |

Verbs such as *want, like*, among others, have a very limited use in the passive in English. In Spanish, a verb such as **querer** can be used impersonally without a subject or with the reflexive pronoun **se**. **No me quieren invitar** literally means *They don't want to invite me*, but it doesn't have to be *they*; it can be anyone whom I don't want to mention. With **se**, the verb is usually singular:

| | |
|---|---|
| **Se** le **quiere** despedir. | *Someone wants to fire him.* |
| Le **quieren** despedir. | *They want to fire him.* |

The verb **estar** can be used with past participles to emphasize the result of an action (a semi-passive). The sentence **La cocina está pintada** is not passive. In this case, **pintada** functions as an adjective that says something about the looks of the kitchen. The following examples will clarify this:

| La radio **estaba apagada**. | The radio was off. |
| La radio **fue apagada**. | The radio was turned off. |

The first example (semi-passive) says something about the radio. The second example (passive) says something about an action.

The verb *get* is translated using **ser** when it has a passive function:

| Él **fue despedido**. | He got fired. |

EJERCICIO
**7·1**

*Change the following sentences to the passive.*

1. Antonio está pintando las paredes.

   _____

2. Ellos no pudieron terminar el trabajo.

   _____

3. La policía tuvo que repeler las agresiones de los manifestantes.

   _____

4. El nuevo gobierno ha derogado esa ley.

   _____

5. Los fabricantes tendrán que revisar todos los nuevos modelos.

   _____

6. El lechero nos trae la leche a nuestra puerta todos los días.

   _____

7. Acaban de instalar el teléfono.

   _____

8. ¿Qué compraron los vecinos?

_____

9. El director va a expulsar a todos esos alumnos.

_____

10. Ella no habría averiguado la combinación.

_____

*Rewrite the following sentences as in the examples.*

EXAMPLES　　Mi televisor está siendo reparado.

*Me están reparando el televisor.*

Antonio no quiso ser ayudado.

*Antonio no quiso que lo ayudaran.*

Me cortaron el césped.

*Hice que me cortaran el césped.*

1. Quieren cortar esta carretera. (Es probable... )

_____

2. Me corto el pelo una vez cada dos meses. (Me... )

_____

3. Alguien está cortando nuestro césped. (Nos... )

_____

4. Ayer nadie me trajo el periódico. (Ayer no me... )

_____

5. Alguien ha robado mi bicicleta. (Me... )

_____

6. Esta casa necesita que la limpien en profundidad. (Esta casa... )

   _____

7. Tengo la impresión de que alguien nos sigue. (Presiento que nos... )

   _____

8. Ellos no fueron invitados. (No les... )

   _____

9. Elena no quiso ser llevada al hospital. (Elena no quiso que... )

   _____

10. Ayer me cambiaron las ruedas delanteras. (Ayer... )

   _____

EJERCICIO

7·3

*Change the following passive sentences to the active voice. Use impersonal sentences as much as possible.*

1. Carlos está siendo tratado en el hospital.

   _____

2. La pobre mujer fue asaltada dos veces en el mismo día.

   _____

3. Las instalaciones han sido clausuradas por la policía.

   _____

4. Javier no va a poder ser liberado este sábado.

   _____

5. Deberían haber sido corregidos en rojo.

   _____

6. Nadie tenía que haber sido admitido ese día.

   _____

7. Eso fue muy mal fabricado.

   _____

8. Nos está siendo explicada en este momento.

   _____

9. Alguien debería haber sido puesto a controlar la entrada.

   _____

10. Voy a ser nombrado jefe de departamento.

    _____

*Find and correct any mistakes.*

1. Los Gallardo han sido expulsado de su casa por no pagar la hipoteca.

2. El inglés es hablado en casi todo el mundo.

3. Nos la están pintada en este momento.

4. Juan es dicho tener la solución.

5. Esa pared está pintada muy mal.

6. No me quieren dejar usar el ordenador.

7. He sido dicho que espere en la segunda planta.

8. Es supuesto que Antonio fue el que lo hizo.

9. Sólo se ha traducido dos cartas.

10. Le han dicho a Paco que regrese cuanto antes.

*Underline the correct choice. In some cases both answers are possible.*

1. Estas placas **se descubrieron/fueron descubiertas** hacia finales de los ochenta.

2. Las importaciones **han incrementado/han sido incrementadas** en un veinte por ciento.

3. No se nos **ha/han** informado de los nuevos cambios.

4. La instalación está **siendo/estando** revisada.

5. Esos coches **se fabrican/son fabricados** casi a mano.

6. En ese país no **hablan/se habla** ruso.

7. Se **necesita/necesitan** vendedores para el verano.

8. América **descubrió/fue descubierta** en 1492.

9. Las nuevas medidas **entrarán/serán entradas** en vigor el mes que viene.

10. Eso **está yendo a/va a** ser remodelado en breve.

*Translate into English.*

1. Nos están limpiando las alfombras.

_____

2. Ayer me trajeron la compra a casa.

_____

3. Ya no se fabrican coches así.

_____

4. El paciente está siendo operado en este momento.

_____

5. Ya deberían haber sido reparados.

   _____

6. Todas las luces fueron encendidas.

   _____

7. Todas las luces estaban encendidas.

   _____

8. El crimen aún no ha sido investigado.

   _____

*Translate into Spanish.*

1. *Two new houses are going to be built in that area.*

   _____

2. *When did you (**tú**) have your car serviced?*

   _____

3. *She is said to work for that company.*

   _____

4. *He is supposed to be the boss.*

   _____

5. *The children should have been watched over.*

   _____

6. *The lights are still off, but they are going to be turned on very soon.*

   _____

7. *She has her dresses made in New York.*

   _____

8. *He should have it looked into by a specialist.*

   _____

9. *Nobody will be allowed to get in without a ticket.*

   _____

10. *Mari can't have been seen there.*

    _____

# Relative pronouns and conjunctions

This unit offers the necessary linking elements in order to make longer speech units and to join related thought patterns. The following relative pronouns and conjunctions will enable you to make your Spanish a lot more interesting.

## Relative pronouns

The most common relative pronoun is **que** (without an accent), which means *that, which,* or *who/whom*:

| | |
|---|---|
| La chica **que** vi ayer... | *The girl (that/whom) I saw yesterday . . .* |
| Juan, **que** es médico, ... | *Juan, who is a doctor, . . .* |
| Ésa es la casa **que** quiero comprar. | *That is the house (that) I want to buy.* |

Spanish relative pronouns can't be omitted.

In English, combinations of the type *at which, with whom,* and so on are used in formal language. In everyday speech, the relative pronoun is usually omitted and the preposition is often put at the end of the clause. A sentence like *That is the man for whom I work* turns into *That is the man I work for.* This type of change is impossible in Spanish. The preposition must precede the relative pronoun. When the pronoun is preceded by a preposition, it is very common to use articles between the pronoun and the preposition:

| | |
|---|---|
| Ésta no es la chica **con la que** me viste. | *This is not the girl you saw me with.* |
| Los hombres **para los que** trabajo son... | *The men I work for are . . .* |

**Chica** is feminine singular, so **la** is used. **Hombres** is masculine plural, therefore **los** is used.

The relative pronoun **quien** (*who/whom*), without an accent, is used with people but not with animals or things. Articles are never used with **quien**:

| | |
|---|---|
| La mujer **con quien** hablé... | *The woman I talked with/with whom I spoke . . .* |
| El hombre **a quien** invitaste... | *The man (that/whom) you invited . . .* |

The transitive verb **invitar** requires the preposition **a** in the above example and in other cases when there is a *direct object* (it tells who is invited, and that person is the direct object of the verb). In these cases, **que** can be used without the definite article, but the preposition **a** is dropped. This applies to all transitive verbs that require the preposition **a**:

| | |
|---|---|
| La mujer **a quien** vi... | *The woman I saw . . .* |
| La mujer **a la que** vi... | *The woman I saw . . .* |
| La mujer **que** vi... | *The woman I saw . . .* |

However, when **que** introduces an indirect object, the article and the preposition **a** cannot be omitted:

| | |
|---|---|
| La mujer **a la que** enviaste las flores... | *The woman you sent the flowers to/ to whom you sent the flowers . . .* |
| La mujer **a quien** enviaste las flores... (*not*: La mujer que enviaste las flores... ) | *The woman you sent the flowers to/ to whom you sent the flowers . . .* |

**Quienes** is used instead of **quien** when the reference is plural:

| | |
|---|---|
| Los hombres **a quienes** invitaste... | *The men you invited . . .* |

**Quien(es)** can be used after a comma, but **que** is more common:

| | |
|---|---|
| Luis, **quien** es arquitecto, ... | *Luis, who is an architect, . . .* |

When there is no comma, it is not possible to use **quien** if the verb doesn't require a preposition:

| | |
|---|---|
| El hombre **que** estuvo aquí... (*not*: El hombre quien estuvo aquí... ) | *The man who was here . . .* |

**El cual, la cual, los cuales**, and **las cuales** can also be used instead of **que/quien(es)** after a comma:

| | |
|---|---|
| Los padres de Rosa, **los cuales** viven... | *Rosa's parents, who live . . .* |
| El señor Robinson, **el cual** está... | *Mr. Robinson, who is . . .* |

These expressions can be used to refer to animals and things as well as people. When there is no comma, they are very common after prepositions:

La tienda **en la cual** compré esto...      *The shop in which/where I bought this . . .*

The masculine noun **motivo** (*reason*) and the feminine noun **razón** (*reason*) are used in the constructions **el motivo por el que/por el cual** or **la razón por la que/por la cual** to translate *the reason* (*why*):

Ése es **el motivo por el que** lo hice.      *That is the reason (why) I did it.*
**La razón por la cual** vine es...      *The reason (why) I came is . . .*

It is not possible to omit **razón** or **motivo** as in the English construction *that's (the reason) why*, although **por qué** (*why*) can be used as a masculine singular noun, requiring the masculine definite article:

Ése es **el por qué** lo hice.      *That's why I did it.*

The relative pronoun **cuyo** means *whose*. It must agree in gender and number with the noun that follows it:

Mis amigos, **cuya madre** está enferma, ...      *My friends, whose mother is ill, . . .*
El chico **cuyo padre** estuvo aquí...      *The boy whose father was here . . .*

The neuter article **lo** can precede the pronoun **que** to mean *what*:

No sé **lo que** voy a hacer.      *I don't know what I'm going to do.*
No me gustó **lo que** vi.      *I didn't like what I saw.*

**Lo cual** can be used instead of **lo que** after a comma:

Juan aprobó todos los exámenes, **lo cual**      *Juan passed all the exams, which*
     me sorprendió.      *surprised me.*

Although **donde** (*where*) and **cuando** (*when*) are considered to be relative adverbs by some grammarians, they function as relative pronouns in linking clauses. The uses of **donde** are very similar to the uses of *where* in English:

Ésa es la casa **donde** nací.      *That is the house where I was born.*
Ésta es la cabina **desde donde** te llamé.      *This is the telephone booth from which/*
     *where I phoned you.*

In such contexts, **donde** can be replaced by constructions with prepositions, articles, and the relative pronouns **que** and **cual**:

Ésta es la casa **en la que** la conocí.      *This is the house in which/where I*
     *met her.*
Éste es el lugar **desde el cual** te vi.      *This is the place from which I saw you.*

As a relative pronoun, **cuando** has a limited use. It can't be used in constructions such as *the year when*. . . . In such cases, **que** is normally used in Spanish:

> Ana se marchó el año **que** vine.      *Ana left the year (when/that) I came.*

It is possible to use the construction **en** + definite article + **que** instead of **que** alone, but in speech **que** alone is much more common:

> La mañana (en la) **que** vine estaba lloviendo.      *The morning that I came it was raining.*

**Cuando** is very common after commas:

> Nací en 1945, **cuando** terminó la guerra.      *I was born in 1945, when the war ended.*

# Conjunctions

Conjunctions are linking words that join clauses or sentences. Correct usage of them will make it possible to create complex constructions that make communication much more interesting. This section offers extensive coverage of English conjunctions and their equivalent forms in Spanish.

## Although/though

Both conjunctions translate as **aunque**:

> **Aunque** está muy lejos de mi casa, me gusta ir allí.      *Although/Though it is a long way from my house, I like going there.*

In English, *though* is often placed at the end of a clause. When this is the case, its common translation is **sin embargo**, which is usually placed at the beginning of the equivalent clause in Spanish. Compare:

> Ella dice que vendrá, **aunque** no creo que lo haga.      *She says she will come, though I don't think she will.*
>
> Ella dice que vendrá; **sin embargo**, no creo que lo haga.      *She says she will come; I don't think she will, though.*

## And

This conjunction translates as **y**:

> Ella habla inglés **y** francés.      *She speaks English and French.*
>
> Trabajo para ella **y** para él.      *I work for her and for him.*

**Y** becomes **e** when it precedes a word that begins with **i**:

Visité Francia **e Inglaterra**.      *I visited France and England.*

## As

In English, *as* is used when the second action takes place before the first is finished. In Spanish, **cuando** is used. To give the impression that the first action has just been completed, **justo cuando** and (**justo**) **en el momento en que** can be used as well:

**Justo cuando** entraba en el edificio,      *As (or: Just as) I entered the building I*
oí la explosión.      *heard the explosion.*

With this meaning, progressive tenses are common in both languages:

Cuando **estaba entrando** en el edificio...      *As I was entering the building . . .*

For parallel actions, *as* translates as **cuando** and **mientras** (*while*). In the past, the imperfect or the imperfect progressive are required:

Ella escuchaba las noticias **cuando/**      *She listened to the news as she cleaned/*
**mientras limpiaba**.      *while she was cleaning.*

For parallel development, *as* translates as **a medida que**. In the past, the imperfect is the most common tense used:

A medida que **pasaba** el tiempo, ella se      *As time went by, she felt better.*
sentía mejor.

In informal Spanish, **conforme** is often used instead of **a medida que**.

When *as* has the same meaning as *while*, its translation is **cuando** or **mientras**. In past narration, it is advisable to use the imperfect or the imperfect progressive:

Mi mujer preparó la cena **mientras/**      *My wife prepared dinner as I was*
**cuando me duchaba**.      *having a shower.*

When the clause with *as* is followed by a verb that implies an action with a (very) short duration, **cuando** is preferable:

**Cuando entraba** (o: **estaba entrando**)      *As I was going into the post office, I saw*
en Correos, vi a Jorge.      *Jorge.*

When *as* has the same meaning as *because/since*, it translates as **como** (without an accent):

| **Como** mi mujer estaba enferma, no pudimos ir a la fiesta. | *As/Since my wife was ill, we couldn't go to the party.* |
|---|---|

If the reason is not mentioned first, **como** is not possible. **Porque** (*because*) and **ya que/puesto que** (*since*) are used instead:

| No pudimos ir a la fiesta, **ya que** mi mujer estaba enferma. (O: ... **puesto que/ porque** mi mujer estaba enferma). | *We couldn't go to the party because my wife was sick.* |
|---|---|

It is even possible to use **pues** for *as/because* in these cases.

*As* translates as **de** with nouns in sentences that refer to periods in a person's life:

| **De niño** tuve muchos problemas de salud. | *As a child I had a lot of health problems.* |
|---|---|

**Como** is common in sentences that talk about duty, responsibility, type of job, and so on:

| **Como hombre casado**, no puedes salir con tus amigos de noche. | *As a married man, you can't go out with your friends at night.* |
|---|---|
| María trabaja **como cajera** en un gran supermercado. | *María works as a cashier in a big supermarket.* |

When talking about the type of job/activity, **de** is possible as well:

| Paco trabaja **de secretario** en un despacho. | *Paco works as a secretary in an office.* |
|---|---|

If the sentence is making a *comparison*, the indefinite article must be used with **como**. Compare:

| Ella trabaja **de/como enfermera**. | *She works as a nurse. (meaning that she is a nurse)* |
|---|---|
| Ella trabaja **como una enfermera**. | *She works like a nurse. (in a similar way, as a nurse would)* |

In English, *as* can mean *though* in constructions such as *Sleepy as he was* .... With this meaning, *as* must be translated as **aunque** or **a pesar de que**:

| **Aunque** él estaba muy cansado, siguió corriendo. | *Tired as he was, he went on running.* |
|---|---|

# Besides

As a conjunction, *besides* translates as **además**:

| No tengo tiempo para ir a esa fiesta; **además**, no me gustan algunos de los invitados. | *I don't have time to go to that party; besides, I don't like some of the guests.* |
|---|---|

| No quiero que vengan; **además**, no hay suficiente comida. | I don't want them to come; besides, there isn't enough food. |

Similar conjunctions are *moreover*, which translates as **además** as well, and *anyway* or *in any case*, which can be translated as **de todas formas**, **de cualquier forma**, **de todos modos**, or **en todo caso**. All these conjunctions could be used in the examples above.

*Besides* can also be a preposition. When this is the case, the preposition **de** is used with **además**:

| **Además de** ser un buen estudiante, trabaja en una gasolinera. | Besides being a good student, he works at a gas station. |

# Both . . . and

The common translation of *both . . . and* is **tanto... como**:

| **Tanto** María **como** Luis aprobaron el examen. | Both María and Luis passed the exam. |
| Visité **tanto** el museo **como** el palacio. | I visited both the museum and the palace. |

In everyday Spanish, this conjunction isn't used as often as *both . . . and* in English. In most cases, Spanish-speaking people prefer constructions with **y**:

| Visité el museo **y** el palacio. | I visited the museum and the palace. |

# But

When *but* is used with a similar meaning to *however*, it is translated as **pero**:

| Ella estuvo en Londres, **pero** no pudo ver a la reina. | She was in London, but she wasn't able to see the queen. |
| Él es bajito **pero** fuerte. | He is short but strong. |

However, when *but* is used to correct information or possible misunderstandings, it must be translated as **sino**:

| Ella no es enfermera, **sino** secretaria. | She isn't a nurse but rather a secretary. |

# Either . . . or/neither . . . nor

The conjunction *either . . . or* translates as **o... o** when the sentence is affirmative:

| Viven **o** en esta calle **o** en ésa. | They live either on this street or on that one. |

As in English, the first part of the conjunction can be left out:

Viven en esta calle **o** en esa.   *They live on this street or on that one.*

When the verb form is negative, **ni** must be used:

Ella no habla inglés **ni** francés.   *She doesn't speak (either) English or French.*

The conjunction **o** becomes **u** when the following word begins with an **o**:

o Nueva York **u Orlando**   *either New York or Orlando*

**Ni... ni** corresponds to the English conjunction *neither . . . nor*:

Ella **no** habla **ni** inglés **ni** francés.   *She speaks neither English nor French.*

Note that a double negative is commonly used, except when **ni** is placed before the verb:

Ella **ni** habla ingles **ni** francés.   *She speaks neither English nor French.*

If a verb takes a preposition (e.g., **hablar con**, **ir a**), the first component of the conjunction is always placed before that preposition:

Tienes que hablar **o con** el director **o con** tu profesor.   *You have to talk either with the principal or with your teacher.*

## For

When *for* is used as a conjunction, explaining something, its common translation is **pues**:

Ella estaba preocupada, **pues** su hijo no había venido todavía.   *She was worried, for her son hadn't come back yet.*

**Pues** has the same limitations as *for* in English. When in doubt, use **porque** (*because*), as both conjunctions have nearly the same meaning:

Ella estaba preocupada **porque** su hijo no había venido todavía.   *She was worried because her son hadn't come back yet.*

## However

As a conjunction, *however* can be translated as **sin embargo** or **no obstante**:

| No estudié mucho el trimestre pasado. **Sin embargo**, aprobé todos los exámenes. | *I didn't study hard last quarter. However, I passed all the exams.* |
|---|---|

As an adverb of degree (e.g., *however hard you studied*), its translation is **no importar lo**, followed by adjectives/adverbs and subjunctive forms:

| Nunca aprobé los exámenes de matemáticas, **no importaba lo** mucho que estudiara. | *I never passed the math tests, however hard I studied.* |
|---|---|

## In spite of/despite

Both forms translate as **a pesar de**, here followed by the infinitive:

| **A pesar de** no tener tiempo, María me ayudó con las cajas. | *In spite of having no time, María helped me with the boxes.* |
|---|---|

This conjunction (and similar ones) can be followed by the relative pronoun **que** and conjugated verbs, whereas English has to use *the fact that*:

| Ella me ayudó con las cajas **a pesar de que** (ella) no tenía tiempo. | *She helped me with the boxes in spite of the fact that she didn't have any time.* |
|---|---|

**A pesar de** can be followed by nouns:

| **A pesar de mi gran esfuerzo**, no pude aprobar el examen. | *In spite of my great effort, I couldn't pass the exam.* |
|---|---|

## Not only . . . but also

This combination translates as **no sólo/solamente... sino también**:

| **No sólo** adultos, **sino también** niños, fueron arrestados por la policía. | *Not only adults but also children were arrested by the police.* |
|---|---|

In the second part of this conjunction, the relative pronoun **que** must be used if the verb sequence is repeated:

| Elena **no sólo** compró la blusa, **sino que también** compró los pantalones. | *Elena not only bought the blouse but also (bought) the trousers.* |
|---|---|

## Or

In affirmative sentences, *or* is translated as **o**:

| Dale esto a Pedro **o** a Antonio. | *Give this to Pedro or to Antonio.* |
|---|---|

When the sentence is negative, English can use *or*, but Spanish has to use **ni**:

Ella **no** trabaja **ni** estudia.         *She doesn't work or study.*

## Otherwise

This conjunction can be translated as **de lo contrario** or as **si no** (*if not*):

| | |
|---|---|
| Debemos darnos prisa; **de lo contrario**, perderemos el tren. | *We must hurry up; otherwise we'll miss the train.* |

The conjunction **de lo contrario** can be replaced by **o**:

| | |
|---|---|
| Debemos darnos prisa, **o** perderemos el tren. | *We must hurry up or (else) we will miss the train.* |

As an adverb, *otherwise* is translated as **de otra forma** or as **de otro modo**:

| | |
|---|---|
| Si lo calculas **de otra forma**, no obtendrás el resultado correcto. | *If you calculate it otherwise, you won't obtain the correct result.* |

## Since

When it functions as a conjunction, *since* is usually translated as **ya que**:

| | |
|---|---|
| Martín no pudo aprobar los exámenes, **ya que** no había estudiado mucho. | *Martín couldn't pass the exams, since he hadn't studied very hard.* |

At the beginning of a sentence it is much better to use **como**:

| | |
|---|---|
| **Como** no tenemos dinero, no iremos de vacaciones este año. | *Since we don't have any money, we won't go on vacation this year.* |

As an adverb, *since* translates as **desde** (**que**):

| | |
|---|---|
| Tengo este reloj **desde** 1958. | *I have had this watch since 1958.* |
| La conozco **desde que** éramos niños. | *I have known her since we were children.* |

## So

As a conjunction to explain something, *so* translates as **así que**:

| | |
|---|---|
| Estaba lloviendo, **así que** nos quedamos en casa. | *It was raining, so we stayed at home.* |

As an adverb of degree, *so* translates as **tan**:

| | |
|---|---|
| Ella es **tan** guapa... | *She is so beautiful . . .* |

## Still/yet

Both conjunctions can be translated as **sin embargo**:

| | |
|---|---|
| Su enfermedad es muy grave; **sin embargo**, hay alguna esperanza. | *His disease is very serious; still, there is some hope.* |
| Era extremadamente peligroso; **sin embargo**, lo hice. | *It was extremely dangerous; yet I did it.* |

When the preceding sentence or clause conveys a negative or difficult characteristic, **no obstante** (*nevertheless* or *all the same*) can be used as well:

| | |
|---|---|
| Ella dijo que era demasiado caro; **no obstante**, lo compró. | *She said it was too expensive; yet/ nevertheless she bought it.* |

**No obstante** can be used in the first two examples also.

*Still* and *yet* can function as adverbs. In this case, *still* translates as **aún** or **todavía**; *yet* translates as **ya** in interrogative sentences and as **aún no/todavía no** in negative sentences:

| | |
|---|---|
| ¿Has terminado **ya**? | *Have you finished yet?* |
| No, **aún** no he terminado. | *No, I haven't finished yet.* |
| **Todavía/Aún** estoy trabajando en ello. | *I'm still working on it.* |

## Therefore

This conjunction can be translated as **por tanto** or **por consiguiente**:

| | |
|---|---|
| No tenemos mucho dinero; **por tanto**, no podemos ir de vacaciones este año. | *We don't have much money; therefore, we can't go on vacation this year.* |

**Por tanto** and **por consiguiente** can be positioned in various places in a sentence, like their English equivalents:

| | |
|---|---|
| No podemos, **por tanto**, ir de vacaciones. | *We can't, therefore, go on vacation.* |
| **Por tanto**, no hemos podido ir. | *Therefore, we haven't been able to go.* |

## When

The equivalent Spanish conjunction is **cuando**:

| | |
|---|---|
| ¿Cómo puedes esperar que te ayude **cuando** tú nunca haces nada por mí? | *How can you expect me to help you when you never do anything for me?* |

In this type of sentence, **cuando** can be replaced by **si** and **mientras** (**que**).

# While

This conjunction is usually translated as **mientras**:

Sucedió **mientras** dormíamos arriba.   *It happened while we were sleeping upstairs.*

Nos robaron **mientras** dábamos un paseo.   *We were robbed while we were taking a walk.*

**Mientras** can be used to emphasize a contrast:

Ella trabaja duramente **mientras** su hermano malgasta el dinero.   *She works hard while her brother wastes money.*

In this case, it is common to add the relative pronoun **que** to **mientras**:

Ella trabaja y estudia **mientras que** su hermano no hace nada.   *She works and studies while her brother doesn't do anything.*

**Mientras** cannot be used to mean *although*. The conjunction **aunque** must be used instead:

**Aunque** me gusta tu oferta, no voy a cambiar de trabajo.   *While I like your offer, I'm not going to change jobs.*

EJERCICIO
8·1

*Fill in the blanks with a correct relative pronoun.*

1. Ésas son las chicas con las _____ estoy en clases de español.

2. El hombre _____ hija estuvo aquí quiere verte.

3. Estuve hablando con el señor Salcedo, _____ es especialista en esta materia.

4. Aún no sé _____ me voy a poner esta noche.

5. Carlos nos invitó a su aniversario, _____ me dio mucha alegría.

6. Eso es algo sin _____ no puedo trabajar.

7. Tomás es el hombre de _____ recibiste las flores.

*Join the following sentences with relative pronouns. Make changes if necessary.*

1. Carla es la doctora. Ella me atendió el otro día.

   _____

2. Antonio quiere ser veterinario. Él adora los animales.

   _____

3. El señor Sánchez vendrá mañana. Yo trabajé para él el año pasado.

   _____

4. Mi profesor de español me ha regalado este libro. Él es muy simpático.

   _____

5. Ése es el coche. Yo gané la carrera con él.

   _____

6. El bar era muy ruidoso. Yo te llamé desde ese bar.

   _____

7. En diciembre organizamos una gran fiesta. Hubo hasta payasos.

   _____

*Join the following sentences by means of suitable conjunctions. Make changes if necessary.*

1. Los resultados de este año han sido muy malos. Esperamos mejorar el año que viene.

   _____

2. No necesito ayuda de nadie. Puedes echarme una mano.

   _____

3. Marta no tenía nada de dinero. Compró un anillo de diamantes.

   _____

4. Entraré en esa discoteca. Es posible que el portero se pelee conmigo.

   _____

5. Ella no pudo conseguir ese empleo. Tenía más de cincuenta años.

   _____

6. Paco no pudo jugar el partido. Tenía una grave lesión.

   _____

7. Yo estaba dando un paseo por el parque. Justo en ese momento cayó el helicóptero.

   _____

EJERCICIO
8·4

*Find and correct any mistakes.*

1. Juan ya no sale, porque es muy mayor.

2. Sin embargo ella es muy mayor, entrena seis horas diarias.

3. Juan no invitó a Tomás, pues eran muy amigos.

4. Ya que no tengo nada que hacer, me voy al cine.

5. A pesar de los temporales, las carreteras están muy bien.

6. No necesito ese préstamo; no obstante, no pienso pedirlo.

7. Porque no me gusta comer fuera de casa, no voy nunca a restaurantes.

*Fill in the blanks with suitable conjunctions.*

1. _____ las condiciones no son muy buenas, pienso aceptar el contrato.

2. Felipe consiguió llegar a la meta _____ que tenía el tobillo muy mal.

3. _____ has terminado tan pronto, ¿por qué no nos tomamos unas copas?

4. El avión aterrizó muy bien _____ su grave avería.

5. Terminé todos los ejercicios, _____ el profesor aún no los había explicado.

6. Mis hijos estudiarán en la universidad _____ yo tenga que trabajar el doble.

7. _____ que pasan los años, pierdo cada vez más memoria.

8. Ella no conoce _____ a Pedro _____ a Juan.

9. Te has portado muy mal; _____ te quedarás sin postre.

10. _____ nuestras enormes dificultades, llegamos a la cima antes que ellos.

*Translate into English.*

1. A pesar de la lluvia, conseguimos terminar el partido de tenis.

_____

2. Aún no he abierto los regalos.

_____

3. Juan no sabía lo que había pasado; así que él no llamó a la policía.

_____

4. A pesar de que era muy tarde, los niños no se fueron a casa.

_____

5. Ni Juan ni Luis habían estado con ella.

_____

6. Tanto Alicia como Pedro visitaron a Roberto en el hospital.

_____

7. Además de tener un yate, Paco tiene un avión.

_____

8. Ella no es enfermera, sino médico.

_____

9. El tiempo estaba horrible; sin embargo, decidimos ir a las montañas.

_____

10. La chica con la que me viste en el restaurante es una hermana de Pablo.

_____

EJERCICIO
8·7

*Translate into Spanish.*

1. *Paco didn't go to the restaurant, since he thought he wasn't wearing the right clothes.*

_____

2. *Both Felipe and Andrea had to repeat the exam.*

_____

3. *Besides working in this hospital, Juan works in a private clinic.*

_____

4. *Either Madrid or Paris will organize the next Olympic Games.*

   _____

5. *We have had this car since we came to live here.*

   _____

6. *Paco can't have seen anything, since he wasn't there at the moment.*

   _____

7. *I don't have much time; however, I will help you.*

   _____

8. *Tomás, who is an architect, will design our new house.*

   _____

9. *Mr. González, for whom I work, is coming to dinner tonight.*

   _____

10. *The woman whose husband applied for the job wants to see you.*

   _____

# Reported speech

When a speaker wants to report what someone said, he or she can use direct or reported (indirect) speech. In direct speech, the speaker gives the exact words that the person said:

Ella dijo, "Hola, ¿cómo estás?"  *She said, "Hello, how are you?"*
Él exclamó, "¡Esta casa es  *He exclaimed, "This house is*
muy fea!"  *very ugly!"*

In reported speech, the speaker changes some of the words that the person said:

Direct Speech: Pedro le dijo  *Pedro said to Antonio, "I have been*
a Antonio, "He estado  *eating with some friends."*
comiendo con unos amigos."

Reported Speech: Pedro le dijo  *Pedro said to Antonio (or: told*
a Antonio que él había  *Antonio) that he had been*
estado comiendo con unos  *eating with some friends.*
amigos.

Direct Speech: Mari le dijo a  *Mari said to Francisco, "My parents*
Francisco, "Mis padres van  *are going to buy a house on the*
a comprar una casa en la  *beach."*
playa."

Reported Speech: Mari le dijo  *Mari told Francisco that her*
a Francisco que sus padres  *parents were going to buy a*
iban a comprar una casa  *house on the beach.*
en la playa.

When a past reporting verb is used (e.g., **dijo**), the tense in reported speech normally changes:

Direct Speech: Mari le dijo a  *Mari said to her father, "I think*
su padre, "**Creo** que **estoy**  *that I'm sick."*
enferma."

Reported Speech: Mari le dijo  *Mari told her father that she*
a su padre que ella **creía**  *thought that she was sick.*
que **estaba** enferma.

| Direct Speech: Ella me dijo, "Te **voy** a comprar un piano para tu cumpleaños." | She told me, "I am going to buy you a piano for your birthday." |
| Reported Speech: Ella me dijo que (ella) me **iba** a comprar un piano para mi cumpleaños. | She told me (that) she was going to buy me a piano for my birthday. |

But when a present reporting verb is used (e.g., **dice**), the tense does not change:

| Direct Speech: Mari le dice a Jorge, "No me **gusta** el barrio en el que **vives**." | Mari says to Jorge, "I don't like the neighborhood you live in." |
| Reported Speech: Mari le dice a Jorge que a ella no le **gusta** el barrio en el que él **vive**. | Mari says to Jorge that she doesn't like the neighborhood he lives in. |

This unit covers all possible changes that occur when reporting someone's speech.

# Tense changes with past reporting verbs

In reported speech, the simple present changes to the imperfect, never to the past perfect:

| Direct Speech: Ella le dijo a él, "Yo no **bebo** café porque **es** malo para mi tensión arterial." | She told him, "I don't drink coffee because it's bad for my blood pressure." |
| Reported Speech: Ella le dijo a él que no **bebía** café porque **era** malo para su tensión arterial. | She told him that she didn't drink coffee because it was bad for her blood pressure. |
| Direct Speech: Yo le dije a ella, "No **necesito** el coche para ir al supermercado." | I told her, "I don't need the car to go to the supermarket." |
| Reported Speech: Yo le dije a ella que yo no **necesitaba** el coche para ir al supermercado. | I told her that I didn't need the car to go to the supermarket. |

The present subjunctive changes to the imperfect subjunctive:

| Direct Speech: Ella me dijo a mí, "No **creo** que mis padres **acepten** eso." | She told me, "I don't think that my parents will accept that." |
| Reported Speech: Ella me dijo a mí que ella no **creía** que sus padres **aceptaran** eso. | She told me that she didn't think that her parents would accept that. |

The imperfect (indicative or subjunctive) and the conditional never change:

| Direct Speech: Yo les dije, "Mi mujer **vivía** en Los Ángeles cuando **era** una niña." | I told them, "My wife lived in Los Angeles when she was a girl." |

| | |
|---|---|
| Reported Speech: Yo les dije que mi mujer **vivía** en Los Ángeles cuando **era** una niña. | *I told them that my wife lived (or: used to live) in Los Angeles when she was a girl.* |
| Direct Speech: Él me dijo, "Si yo **tuviera** dinero, (yo) **compraría** un castillo." | *He told me, "If I had money, I would buy a castle."* |
| Reported Speech: Él me dijo que si él **tuviera** dinero, (él) **compraría** un castillo. | *He told me that if he had money, he would buy a castle.* |

The preterit can change to the past perfect, but it can also remain in the preterit:

| | |
|---|---|
| Direct Speech: Ella le dijo a él, "Yo no **estuve** en la casa de mis padres." | *She told him, "I wasn't in my parents' house."* |
| Reported Speech: Ella le dijo (a él) que ella no **había estado** en la casa de sus padres. (O: Ella le dijo [a él] que ella no **estuvo**... ) | *She told him that she hadn't been in her parents' house.* |

The future tense changes to the conditional:

| | |
|---|---|
| Direct Speech: Yo les dije, "No **iré** con vosotros a esa fiesta tan extraña." | *I told them, "I won't go with you to such a strange party."* |
| Reported Speech: Yo les dije que (yo) no **iría** con ellos a esa fiesta tan extraña. | *I told them that I wouldn't go with them to such a strange party.* |

The conditional doesn't change:

| | |
|---|---|
| Direct Speech: Yo le dije a mi madre, "Me **gustaría** tener una moto." | *I said to my mother, "I would like to have a motorcycle."* |
| Reported Speech: Yo le dije a mi madre que me **gustaría** tener una moto. | *I told my mother that I would like to have a motorcycle.* |

In reported speech, after the reporting verb (e.g., **dijo**), there is a clause with a verb sequence. As only the first verb in the verb sequence can change, it doesn't make any sense to learn how complex verb sequences (two or more verbs together) behave. In the sentence **Ellos han estado comiendo en ese restaurante**, the only verb that can change is **han**; the verbs following remain unchanged. Supposing that a girl called Marta said this, the reported speech would be **Marta dijo que ellos habían estado comiendo en ese restaurante**. In other words, you only have to change (or not) the first verb of the verb sequence in accordance with the previous rules, without worrying about the tense being perfect, conditional perfect, and so on:

| | |
|---|---|
| Direct Speech: Yo les dije, "Ellos **habrán estado jugando** al fútbol." | *I told them, "They must have been playing soccer."* |

| | |
|---|---|
| Reported Speech: Yo les dije que ellos **habrían estado jugando** al fútbol. | *I told them that they might have been playing soccer.* |
| Direct Speech: Ella le dijo a su padre, "No **me voy a poder** poner ese vestido." | *She said to her father, "I'm not going to be able to put on that dress."* |
| Reported Speech: Ella le dijo a su padre que no **se iba a poder** poner ese vestido. | *She told her father that she wasn't going to be able to put on that dress.* |

In reporting something that is still true, the first verb of the verb sequence (that is, after the reporting verb) doesn't have to be changed:

| | |
|---|---|
| Ella dijo que Juan **tiene/tenía** dos niños. | *She said that Juan has two children.* |

But the tense is always changed when there is a difference between what was said and what is really the case:

| | |
|---|---|
| Ella dijo que Juan **tenía** dos niños, pero en realidad **tiene** tres. | *She said that Juan had two children, but in fact he has three.* |

The construction **puede que** + present subjunctive changes to **podía que** + imperfect subjunctive or to **podía/podría** + infinitive:

| | |
|---|---|
| Direct speech: Él dijo, "**Puede que** llueva mañana." | *He said, "It may rain tomorrow."* |
| Reported speech: Él dijo que **podía que lloviera** al día siguiente. (O: Él dijo que **podía/podría llover** al día siguiente.) | *He said that it might rain the following day.* |

The construction **podía ser** + imperfect subjunctive is also possible in this case.

# Changes in pronouns, adjectives, adverbs, and other parts of speech

As you have already seen, when the person reporting speaks in a different place or at a different time, there are other changes apart from tense changes. Words like **aquí**, **ahora**, **mañana**, and so on need to be changed if the person reporting is in a different place at a period of time after the reported sentence was originally said. Following are common changes:

| Direct Speech | Reported Speech |
|---|---|
| aquí/acá | allí/allá |
| esta mañana/tarde/noche | esa/aquella mañana/tarde/noche |

| | |
|---|---|
| hoy | ese/aquel día |
| mañana | al día siguiente |
| ayer | el día antes/anterior |
| el lunes que viene | al lunes siguiente |
| la semana que viene | a la semana siguiente |
| el/la... que viene | al/a la... siguiente |
| hace un año | hacía un año |
| hace + tiempo | hacía + tiempo |
| este, esta, esto | ese/aquel, esa/aquella, eso/aquello |
| estos, estas | esos/aquellos, esas/aquellas |

Demonstratives can also change to definite articles in reported speech. Possessives and object pronouns depend on the person(s) talked about in the narration:

| | |
|---|---|
| Direct Speech: Ella le dijo a Tomás, "**Hoy** no quiero salir." | *She said to Tomás, "I don't want to go out today."* |
| Reported Speech: Ella le dijo a Tomás que no quería salir **ese día**. (Or: Ella le dijo a Tomás que **ese día** no quería salir.) | *She told Tomás that she didn't want to go out that day.* |
| Direct Speech: Yo te dije a ti, "**Esto** no es asunto tuyo." | *I told you, "This is none of your business."* |
| Reported Speech: Yo te dije que **eso** no era asunto tuyo. | *I told you that that was none of your business.* |
| Direct Speech: Él le dijo a su padre, "**Mañana** no **puedo** ayudarte con la limpieza." | *He said to his father, "I can't help you with the cleaning tomorrow."* |
| Reported Speech: Él le dijo a su padre que no le **podía** ayudar con la limpieza **al día siguiente**. (O: Él le dijo a su padre que no le **podría** ayudar con la limpieza **al día siguiente**.) | *He told his father that he couldn't help him with the cleaning the following day.* |

When the person reporting is in a different place, the verb **venir** can change to **ir**, and the verb **traer** can change to **llevar**:

| | |
|---|---|
| Direct Speech: Yo les dije a mis amigos, "**Tenéis que venir** a mi casa esta noche." | *I said to my friends, "You have to come to my house tonight."* |
| Reported Speech: Yo les dije a mis amigos que **tenían que ir** a mi casa esa noche. | *I told my friends that they had to come to my house that night.* |
| Direct Speech: Yo le dije a María, "**Puedes traer** a tus amigos." | *I said to María, "You can bring your friends."* |
| Reported Speech: Yo le dije a María que **podía llevar** a sus amigos. | *I told María that she could bring her friends.* |

**Traer** (and even **venir**) needn't change when the reporting person is "mentally" situated in the place reported:

Direct Speech: Ella le dijo a él, "**Debes traer** los libros esta noche."

*She said to him, "You must bring the books tonight."*

Reported Speech: Ella le dijo a él que **debía traer/llevar** los libros esa noche.

*She told him that he had to bring the books that night.*

All the previous rules must be applied to independent sentences. This means that words like **que**, **cuando**, **mientras**, **si**, and so on indicate the beginning of another sentence (except **que** in the verb **tener que**).

## Reported questions

The changes explained previously occur when the speaker is reporting interrogative sentences. When there is no interrogative pronoun, **si** (*if*) is used to introduce a reported question. Spanish can use the relative pronoun **que** in reported information questions:

Direct Speech: Ella me preguntó, "¿**Dónde** viven tus padres?"

*She asked me, "Where do your parents live?"*

Reported Speech: Ella me preguntó **que dónde** vivían mis padres.

*She asked me where my parents lived.*

Direct Speech: Juan le dijo a Elena, "¿**Qué** sueles hacer tú los sábados?"

*Juan said to Elena, "What do you usually do on Saturdays?"*

Reported Speech: Juan le preguntó a Elena **que qué** solía ella hacer los sábados.

*Juan asked Elena what she usually did on Saturdays.*

Direct Speech: Yo le dije a María, "¿**Puedes** ayudarme con mis ejercicios?"

*I said to María, "Can you help me with my exercises?"*

Reported Speech: Yo le pregunté a María **si** ella **podía** ayudarme con mis ejercicios.

*I asked María if she could help me with my exercises.*

As you can see, in reported questions inversion of the subject is very frequent.

## Reporting verbs

In addition to **decir** and **preguntar**, many other verbs can be used in reported statements or questions:

| | | | |
|---|---|---|---|
| admitir | *to admit* | advertir de | *to warn* |
| añadir | *to add* | argumentar | *to argue* |

| | | | |
|---|---|---|---|
| asegurar | to assure | avisar | to inform, notify |
| comentar | to comment, remark | contar | to tell |
| contestar/ responder | to answer | exclamar | to exclaim |
| explicar | to explain | murmurar | to murmur |
| objetar | to object | observar | to observe |
| preguntarse | to wonder | prometer | to promise |
| quejarse de | to complain | querer saber | to want to know |
| recordar | to remember, remind | | |

Here are some examples:

| | |
|---|---|
| Carlos **añadió que** no le gustaba la película de esa noche. | *Carlos added that he didn't like that night's film.* |
| Ella **explicó que** su marido no había estado en casa ese día. | *She explained that her husband hadn't been at home that day.* |
| Ellos **se quejaron de que** las habitaciones estaban muy sucias. | *They complained that the rooms were very dirty.* |
| Yo les **conté que** vi a esa actriz cuando iba a mi casa. | *I told them that I saw that actress when I was going to my house.* |
| La señora Gálvez **comentó que** las joyas eran muy caras. | *Mrs. Gálvez commented that the jewels were very expensive.* |
| Ella **quiso saber si** yo había visto a Jorge el día antes. | *She wanted to know if I had seen Jorge the day before.* |

These reporting verbs can be used either in the imperfect or in the preterit, but the latter is much more common because the person reporting usually considers the sentence being reported as something finished in the past. In the clause **Ella me comentaba**, the person reporting is referring to the moment at which the sentence was being pronounced. **Ella me comentó** refers simply to the words said in the past.

# Interpreting direct speech

Most sentences said by somebody who wants something to be done can be reported by simply narrating them or by using a verb that "interprets" the attitude or the intentions of the speaker. If my wife said to me, **Creo que deberías cortarte el pelo** (*I think you should have your hair cut*), I can report this to a friend by saying **Mi mujer dijo que ella creía que yo debería cortarme el pelo** (*My wife said that she thought that I should have my hair cut*) or by saying **Mi mujer me aconsejó que me cortara el pelo** (*My wife advised me to have my hair cut*). This second version is an "interpretation" of what I think was my wife's intention. Most "interpretation" verbs must be followed by subjunctive structures.

# Imperatives

Imperatives are usually reported using subjunctive forms:

Direct Speech: El profesor dijo, "**No toquéis** los ordenadores."

*The teacher said, "Don't touch the computers."*

Reported Speech: El profesor (nos) dijo que **no tocáramos** los ordenadores.

*The teacher told us not to touch the computers.*

In addition to the verb **decir**, which can be used in all the following examples, there are many other interpretation verbs to report imperatives, depending on the way the sentence was said and on the speaker's intonation or intentions:

Direct Speech: Ella me dijo, "¡**No entres** en esa habitación sin mi permiso!"

*She said to me, "Don't go into that room without my permission!"*

Reported Speech: Ella me **ordenó que no entrara** en esa habitación sin su permiso.

*She ordered me not to go into that room without her permission.*

Direct Speech: Yo le dije a ella, "Por favor, **dame** ese diccionario."

*I said to her, "Please, give me that dictionary."*

Reported Speech: Yo le **pedí que me diera** ese/el diccionario.

*I asked her to give me that/the dictionary.*

Direct Speech: Mi padre me dijo, "¡**No te acerques** demasiado al filo!"

*My father said to me, "Don't get too near the edge!"*

Reported Speech: Mi padre me **advirtió que no me acercara** demasiado al filo.

*My father warned me not to get too near the edge.*

Direct Speech: Mi amiga Carla me dijo, "**Ven** a mi fiesta esta noche."

*My friend Carla said to me, "Come to my party tonight."*

Reported Speech: Mi amiga Carla me **ofreció que fuera** a su fiesta esa noche. (O: Mi amiga Carla me **invitó a** ir... o: Mi amiga Carla me **invitó a que fuera**...)

*My friend Carla invited me to come to her party that night.*

Direct Speech: Ella le dijo a su marido, "**No olvides** limpiar la cochera mañana."

*She said to her husband, "Don't forget to clean the garage tomorrow."*

Reported Speech: Ella le **recordó** a su marido **que limpiara** la cochera al día siguiente.

*She reminded her husband to clean the garage the next day.*

Direct Speech: Dándome ánimos, Carlos me dijo, "**Estudia** medicina."

*Carlos said to me encouragingly, "Study medicine."*

Reported Speech: Carlos me **animó a estudiar** medicina. (O: Carlos me **animó a que estudiara** medicina.)

*Carlos encouraged me to study medicine.*

Direct Speech: Mi madre me dijo, "Por favor, **ten** mucho cuidado."

*My mother said to me, "Please, be very careful."*

Reported Speech: Mi madre me **rogó que tuviera** mucho cuidado.

*My mother begged me to be very careful.*

First-person plural imperatives can be reported using the verbs **decir de**, **proponer**, and **sugerir**:

| | |
|---|---|
| Direct Speech: Antonio me dijo, "**Vayamos** a Nueva York." | *Antonio said to me, "Let's go to New York."* |
| Reported Speech: Antonio **dijo de ir** a Nueva York. (O: Antonio **propuso/ sugirió ir** a Nueva York.) | *Antonio proposed/suggested going to New York.* |

Subjunctive constructions are possible in the preceding example (**dijo que fuéramos**, **propuso que fuéramos**, **sugirió que fuéramos**), but they could imply that Anthony didn't go to New York after all.

## Advice, suggestions, proposals, and recommendations

Certain elements in the sentence to be reported indicate that the speaker's intentions were to suggest/advise/propose/recommend something:

| | |
|---|---|
| Direct Speech: Ella me dijo, "**Si yo fuera tú**, no compraría en esa tienda." | *She said to me, "If I were you, I wouldn't buy in that shop."* |
| Reported Speech: Ella me **aconsejó/ sugirió/recomendó/propuso que no comprara** en esa tienda. | *She advised me not to buy in that shop. (Or: She suggested/recommended/ proposed that I not buy in that shop.)* |
| Direct Speech: Yo le dije a él, "**Creo que deberías** hablar con tus padres." | *I said to him, "I think that you should talk with your parents."* |
| Reported Speech: Yo le **aconsejé/sugerí/ recomendé/propuse que hablara** con sus padres. | *I advised him to talk with his parents. (Or: I suggested/recommended/ proposed that he talk with his parents.)* |
| Direct Speech: Mi padre me dijo, "**¿Qué tal si nos vamos** a pescar?" | *My father said to me, "How about going fishing?"* |
| Reported Speech: Mi padre **sugirió/ propuso irnos** a pescar. (O: Mi padre **sugirió/propuso que nos fuéramos** a pescar.) | *My father suggested/proposed going fishing.* |
| Direct Speech: Juan le dijo a Ana, "**¿Por qué no dejas** de fumar?" | *Juan said to Ana, "Why don't you give up smoking?"* |
| Reported Speech: Juan le **aconsejó/ sugirió/propuso/recomendó** a Ana **que dejara** de fumar. | *Juan advised Ana to give up smoking. (Or: Juan suggested/recommended/ proposed that Ana give up smoking.)* |

Sentences of the type *Shall I/we* can be reported using **ofrecer** or **ofrecerse a** when the context implies an offer:

Direct Speech: Ellos le dijeron a él,
    "¿**Te ayudamos** con esto?"
Reported Speech: Ellos **ofrecieron
    ayudarle** con eso. (O: Ellos **se
    ofrecieron a ayudarle** con eso.)

*They said to him, "Shall we help you
    with this?"*
*They offered to help him with that.*

Sentences of the type *Shall I/we* can be reported using **proponer** or **sugerir** when the sentence implies a proposal or suggestion:

Direct Speech: Ella le dijo a su hijo,
    "¿**Pedimos** una pizza?"
Reported Speech: Ella le **propuso** a su hijo
    **pedir** una pizza. (O: Ella **sugirió pedir**
    una pizza.)

*She said to her son, "Shall we order
    a pizza?"*
*She proposed/suggested ordering a pizza.*

In this example, a subjunctive construction would not be suitable, as then the reported sentence could imply that it is only the son who orders the pizza.

## Requests

There are many interrogative sentences that clearly indicate that the speaker wants or needs somebody to do something. These sentences can be reported using the verb **pedir** and a subjunctive form:

Direct Speech: Yo le dije a mi profesor,
    "¿**Puede usted explicar** eso de nuevo,
    por favor?"
Reported Speech: Yo le **pedí** a mi profesor
    **que explicara** eso de nuevo.
Direct Speech: Ella le dijo al dependiente,
    "¿**Podría mostrarme** algunos anillos
    más?"
Reported Speech: Ella le **pidió** al
    dependiente **que le mostrara** algunos
    anillos más.

*I said to my teacher, "Can you explain
    that again, please?"*

*I asked my teacher to explain that again.*

*She said to the salesperson, "Could you
    show me some more rings?"*

*She asked the salesperson to show her
    some more rings.*

Sentences with *will you* in English can normally be reported using the verb **pedir** in Spanish:

Direct Speech: Yo le dije al señor Antúnez, "**¿Quiere usted sentarse**, por favor?"

*I said to Mr. Antúnez, "Will you sit down, please?"*

Reported Speech: Yo le **pedí** al señor Antúnez **que se sentara**.

*I asked Mr. Antúnez to sit down.*

However, if a sentence with *will you* in English is spoken sharply or irritably, it can be reported in Spanish using **decir** or **ordenar**:

Direct Speech: Ella le dijo a su alumno, "**¡Quieres abrir** tu libro!"

*She said to her student, "Will you open your book!"*

Reported Speech: Ella le **dijo/ordenó** a su alumno **que abriera** su libro.

*She told/ordered her student to open his book.*

Don't forget that *would*, to make a request, is translated using the conditional of **querer**:

**¿Querrías** callarte?

*Would you be quiet?*

## Exclamations, threats, wishes, congratulations, and deductions

Exclamations can be reported by the verb **exclamar**, but **decir** is more common in everyday Spanish:

Direct Speech: El hombre **dijo**, "¡Qué mujer tan bonita!"

*The man said, "What a pretty woman!"*

Reported Speech: El hombre **exclamó/dijo que** la mujer era muy bonita.

*The man exclaimed/said that the woman was very pretty.*

Threats are reported by the verb **amenazar con** and infinitive forms:

Direct Speech: Yo le **dije** a mi hijo, "Si no haces tus deberes, no verás la tele esta noche."

*I said to my son, "If you don't do your homework, you won't watch TV tonight."*

Reported Speech: **Amenacé** a mi hijo **con** no ver la tele esa noche si no hacía sus deberes.

*I threatened my son with not watching TV that night if he didn't do his homework.*

Wishes are reported by the verb **desear**. This verb can be followed by nouns and by subjunctive forms:

| Direct Speech: Ella le **dijo** a su cliente, "**Que tenga** un buen viaje!" | *She said to her client, "Have a good trip."* |
| Reported Speech: Ella le **deseó** a su cliente **que tuviera** un buen viaje. (O: Ella le **deseó** a su cliente un buen viaje.) | *She wished her client a good trip.* |

Congratulations require **felicitar** or **dar la enhorabuena**. Both are followed by the preposition **por** and infinitive forms or nouns:

| Direct Speech: Mi profesor me **dijo**, "¡Enhorabuena! **Has aprobado** el examen de inglés." | *My teacher said to me, "Congratulations! You've passed your English exam."* |
| Reported Speech: Mi profesor me **felicitó por aprobar/haber aprobado** el examen de inglés. (O: Mi profesor me **dio la enhorabuena por aprobar/haber aprobado** el examen de inglés.) | *My teacher congratulated me on my passing my English exam.* |

Deductions can be reported by **deducir**, **inferir**, **suponer**, among others:

| Direct Speech: El policía dijo, "**Deben de estar** en casa, porque las luces están encendidas." | *The policeman said, "They must be at home, because the lights are on."* |
| Reported Speech: El policía **dedujo que estaban** en casa, porque las luces estaban encendidas. | *The policeman deduced that they were at home, because the lights were on.* |

# Denying and refusing

Sentences in which the subject denies something can be reported by the verb **negar** (followed by the infinitive or subjunctive structures). Refusals are reported by the pronominal verb **negarse a** (followed only by the infinitive):

| Direct Speech: Él dijo, "Yo **no tengo** nada que ver con ese robo." | *He said, "I have nothing to do with that theft."* |
| Reported Speech: Él **negó tener** nada que ver con ese robo. (O: Él **negó que tuviera** nada que ver con ese robo.) | *He denied having anything to do with that theft.* |
| Direct Speech: Ella dijo, "No **participaré** en esa carrera." | *She said, "I won't participate in that race."* |
| Reported Speech: Ella **se negó a participar** en esa carrera. | *She refused to participate in that race.* |

*Imagine you are in a different place and time, and put the following sentences into indirect/reported speech.*

1. Juan le dijo a Antonio, "No me va muy bien con los estudios."

   _____

2. Ella me dijo a mí, "Creo que mañana va a haber una manifestación en esta calle."

   _____

3. Yo le dije a mi novia, "Esta noche no nos podemos ver aquí."

   _____

4. Mi profesor me dijo, "Estos ejercicios tienen que estar hechos para mañana."

   _____

5. Él dijo, "Aún no sé si podré pagar todas estas facturas antes del lunes que viene."

   _____

6. El juez le dijo a él, "Yo le condeno a tres meses de prisión menor."

   _____

7. Ella dijo, "No he estado haciendo nada importante esta tarde."

   _____

8. Yo les dije, "Ayer no estuve en el colegio, porque estaba enfermo."

   _____

*Put the following questions into reported speech. Use the verb* **preguntar** *in all of them.*

1. Juan le dijo a Paco, "¿Con quién vas a pasar esta Navidad?"

   _____

2. Marta me dijo, "¿Ya ha regresado tu hermana?"

   _____

3. Yo les dije, "¿Por qué no pasáis y os tomáis una copa?"

   _____

4. Ella me dijo, "¿En qué universidad estudió tu hermano?"

   _____

5. El policía me dijo, "¿Ha bebido usted mucho esta noche?"

   _____

6. Mi madre me dijo, "¿A qué se debe que estés aquí tan temprano?"

   _____

7. Yo les dije, "¿Os apetece cenar con nosotros?"

   _____

8. El profesor dijo, "¿Quién descubrió América?"

   _____

*Put the following commands into reported speech. Use the verb **decir** in all of them.*

1. Ella me dijo, "Sujeta esto hasta que me baje de la escalera."

   _____

2. Yo les dije, "Hablad más bajito para que no se despierte el bebé."

   _____

3. Pablo me dijo, "No tires de este cable hasta que yo te lo diga."

   _____

4. La enfermera me dijo, "Espere aquí hasta que le llamen por el altavoz."

   _____

5. Ella me dijo, "No vengas mañana."

   _____

6. El profesor nos dijo, "Haced estos ejercicios para la semana que viene."

   _____

7. El profesor nos dijo, "No olvidéis traer el trabajo terminado."

   _____

8. El policía le dijo a mi amigo, "No aparque usted tan pegado a la pared."

   _____

*Put the following sentences into reported speech. Use interpretation verbs.*

1. Yo le dije a él, "¡No quiero que uses mi despacho sin que yo esté aquí!"

   _____

2. Ella le dijo a él, "Pasa y ponte cómodo, por favor."

   _____

3. Él dijo, "Ya deben de ser las seis. Deberíamos irnos."

   _____

4. El ladrón le dijo a su compañero, "¡Alguien viene! ¡Métete en ese armario!"

   _____

5. Yo le dije a ella, "Si yo fuera tú, yo no aceptaría esas condiciones."

   _____

6. Él me dijo a mí, "¿Por qué no te matriculas en la universidad?"

   _____

7. Pablo dijo, "Puede que ella tenga que declarar también."

   _____

8. Él me dijo a mí, "Coge esto y llévalo a la biblioteca, por favor."

   _____

EJERCICIO
9·5

*Put the following sentences into direct speech.*

1. Mi primo me pidió que le echara una mano con la limpieza de los cuartos de baño.

   _____

2. Ella dijo de coger un taxi para ir al centro. (*Use the* nosotros *form.*)

   _____

3. Juan me comentó que sus padres estaban pensando en el divorcio.

   _____

4. Elena me dijo que su marido había tenido que dejar la empresa porque había asuntos sucios.

   _____

5. Carlos dedujo que Antonio tenía más de cuarenta años.

   _____

6. Les ordené que se callaran de inmediato, porque estaba intentando estudiar para el día siguiente.

   _____

7. Mi padre me recordó que fuera a echar las cartas al correo.

   _____

8. Ana me pidió que le sujetara la puerta.

   _____

EJERCICIO
9·6

*Translate into English.*

1. Les sugerí que no fueran a ese barrio.

   _____

2. Mónica me aconsejó que me quedara unos días.

   _____

3. Paco nos pidió que le lleváramos a su casa, porque no se sentía muy bien.

   _____

4. Mi madre me ha prohibido que te vea.

   _____

5. Mi padre me ha prometido que me llevará al zoológico este fin de semana.

   _____

6. Jaime les dijo que no entraran sin quitarse los zapatos primero.

_____

7. Les di la enhorabuena por el nacimiento de su hija.

_____

8. Manolo nos contó que su mujer iba a ser operada al día siguiente.

_____

9. Les pregunté si habían comido alguna vez en ese restaurante.

_____

10. Sara nos suplicó que la ayudáramos a convencer a su marido.

_____

_Translate into Spanish._

1. _She told me not to make so much noise._

_____

2. _He told her to wait there until he came back._

_____

3. _I asked Mari if she felt like having dinner with me._

_____

4. _He denied having written that letter._

_____

5. _Juan refused to take part in the joke._

_____

6. _She ordered me to clean the floor._

_____

7. *Miguel suggested that we visit that city.*

_____

8. *He advised us not to go there by car.*

_____

9. *He forbade us to talk during the exam.*

_____

10. *She said that she hadn't been there the day before.*

_____

# Problematic prepositions I

It is often not possible to say exactly how English prepositions translate, unless attention is paid to the context in which they are used. In order to address this problem, these units are arranged by possible contexts and situations. In a large number of cases, English prepositions are not translated using equivalent Spanish prepositions but by means of prepositional constructions. This unit covers the different translations for *at*, *in*, and *on* and the possible variations depending on the context.

## Location and position

When referring to position and location, the most common translation for *at*, *in*, or *on* is **en**:

| | |
|---|---|
| en el colegio | *at school* |
| en una fiesta | *at a party* |
| en la puerta | *at the door* |
| en el teatro | *at the theater* |
| en el dentista | *at the dentist's* |
| en el fondo | *at the bottom* |
| en la cama | *in bed/on the bed* |
| en el hospital | *in the hospital* |
| en la calle | *in/on the street* |
| en la carretera | *in/on the road* |
| en un barco | *on a ship* |
| en el tejado | *on the roof* |

In English, the preposition *in* is related to interior, *on* is related to surface, and *at* is most commonly used when there is no certain idea of interior or surface. In Spanish, in all the situations above, the common preposition is **en**, although in some cases other prepositions can be used.

149

Dentro de (*inside*) can always replace **en** when referring to position inside or movement into the interior of something:

Están **dentro de** la casa.                      *They are in(side) the house.*

**En la cama** means *in bed* and *on the bed*. **Sobre la cama** can mean only *on the bed*.

With the noun **puerta** you can also use the preposition **a** (**a la puerta**), but this is becoming a little old-fashioned. In the plural, the construction **a las puertas (de)** is a commonly used expression meaning *at the entrance (of/to)* (e.g., a town) or *at the beginning (of)* (e.g., a period of time):

Las tropas estaban **a las puertas de** París.   *The troops were just outside Paris.*
Estamos **a las puertas del** verano.            *It's the beginning of summer.*

With nouns that clearly refer to surface (**tejado**, **suelo**, **mesa**, etc.) you can also use the preposition **sobre**, especially when you want to be very specific:

Los libros están **sobre la mesa**.              *The books are on the table.*
Los niños caminaban **sobre el tejado**.         *The children were walking on the roof.*
Ellos estaban tumbados **sobre el frío suelo**.  *They were lying on the cold floor.*

Certain words referring to surface can be used with **sobre** when *the whole of the surface* is meant. Compare:

un auténtico diluvio **sobre la costa**           *a real deluge on the coast*

**En** is also possible in the above example.

The preposition **en** is advisable when referring to position on a surface:

Ellos compraron una casa **en la costa**.        *They bought a house on the coast.*

**Sobre** is not possible in the example above.

The words **derecha** (*right*) and **izquierda** (*left*) are preceded by the prepositions **a** or **hacia** (**a** is much more frequent):

El banco está **a la derecha**.                  *The bank is on the right.*
Gira **a la derecha**.                           *Turn to the right.*

**Hacia** is also possible in the above examples.

The noun **parte** (*side, part*) needs the preposition **en**:

Las camisas están **en la parte superior**       *The shirts are on the top right-hand side.*
   **derecha**.

The preposition **a** is not possible above.

The noun **lado** (*side, end*) can be used with **a** or **en** to indicate position:

| | |
|---|---|
| Ella estaba sentada **en la otra parte** (o: **en/al otro lado**). | *She was sitting on the other side.* |
| **al otro lado** del teléfono | *on the other end of the phone (line)* |

**Al** is the contraction of the preposition **a** and the article **el**.

You should be aware of the fact that the preposition **a** usually refers to movement toward a place. This means that even the noun **parte** takes **a** when verbs of movement are used:

| | |
|---|---|
| Ella se dirigía **a la parte superior**. | *She was going to/toward the upper part (top).* |
| **Pedro fue al otro lado.** | *Pedro went to the other side.* |

**Hacia** is possible instead of **a** in both of these examples.

The noun **fondo** means *bottom* and *far end*. When it means *bottom*, **en el fondo** is used; when it means *far end*, **al fondo** is used:

| | |
|---|---|
| El submarino está **en el fondo**. | *The submarine is at the bottom.* |
| Tus libros están **en el fondo** de la caja. | *Your books are at the bottom of the box.* |
| Están **al fondo** del pasillo. | *They are at the end of the corridor.* |

**En el fondo** can also be an expression meaning *actually, really,* or *deep down* (figuratively):

| | |
|---|---|
| **En el fondo** soy muy romántico. | *I'm very romantic, actually.* |

**A fondo** is an expression meaning *thoroughly, closely*:

| | |
|---|---|
| Voy a estudiar esto a fondo. | *I'm going to study this closely.* |

**A fondo** is also used to indicate maximum speed. It is related to the accelerator of a car, but it can also be used figuratively:

| | |
|---|---|
| ¡Pisa a fondo! | *Step on it! (Floor it! Press the accelerator to the floor!)* |

The preposition **a** is often used to indicate proximity. Compare:

| | |
|---|---|
| Ella estaba sentada **a la mesa**. | *She was sitting at the table.* |
| Los platos estaban **en/sobre la mesa**. | *The dishes were on the table.* |

Many Spanish-speaking people don't apply this rule of proximity properly; it is very common to hear **Ella estaba sentada en la mesa**, which is colloquial but incorrect.

The English construction **at** + genitive (possessive) (e.g., *at Peter's*) must be translated using **en** and **la casa de** (*the house of*) when a specific home is meant. If no home is referred to, nouns like **bar**, **restaurante**, **tienda**, and so on can be added to be more precise:

| | |
|---|---|
| Voy a comer **en la casa de Juan**. | *I'm going to eat at Juan's (house).* |
| Están **en el bar de Paco**. | *They are at Paco's (bar).* |

Many Spanish bars and restaurants use the noun **Casa** in their names. When this is the case, no articles are used. Compare:

| | |
|---|---|
| Voy a comer **en la casa de Juan**. | *I'm going to eat at Juan's (house).* |
| Ella está **en Casa Juan**. | *She is at Casa Juan. (a restaurant)* |

Other genitive constructions referring to a business are formed using the preposition **en** and either the name of the owner or a specific name for a type of business:

| | |
|---|---|
| en el médico/en la consulta del médico | *at the doctor's* |
| en el dentista/en la consulta del dentista | *at the dentist's* |
| en la farmacia | *at the pharmacy* |
| en la panadería | *at the baker's/bakery* |
| en la carnicería | *at the butcher's/butcher shop* |

*On television* translates as **en la televisión**. The preposition **sobre** refers to the surface of the TV set. Compare:

| | |
|---|---|
| Hay un magnífico programa **en la tele**. | *There is a great program on TV.* |
| He puesto las cartas **sobre la tele**. | *I have put the letters on the TV set.* |

The same applies to other mass media:

| | |
|---|---|
| Lo oí **en la radio**. | *I heard it on the radio.* |
| Lo publiqué **en este periódico**. | *I published it in this newspaper.* |

The preposition **en** is common with nouns that refer to social events or activities:

| | |
|---|---|
| en la boda | *at the wedding* |
| en una fiesta | *at a party* |
| en el trabajo | *at work* |
| en una reunión | *at a meeting* |

# Time and other contexts

Prepositions are not used with days of the week. Use definite articles instead: **los** for general reference and **el** to refer to a specific day of the week:

| | |
|---|---|
| Odio **los lunes**. | *I hate Mondays.* |
| Ella nunca viene **los martes**. | *She never comes on Tuesdays.* |

| | |
|---|---|
| Juan estuvo aquí **el miércoles**. | *Juan was here last Wednesday.* |
| Volveremos **el domingo**. | *We will be back next Sunday.* |

The article **el** is part of two constructions that translate *next* and *last*. **El** + day of the week + **que viene** is the common translation for *next* + day of the week:

| | |
|---|---|
| No jugaremos **el lunes que viene**. | *We won't play next Monday.* |

**El próximo lunes** and **el lunes próximo** are correct, too.

**El** + day of the week + **pasado** translates *last* + day of the week:

| | |
|---|---|
| Ocurrió **el lunes pasado**. | *It happened last Monday.* |

**El pasado lunes** is also correct.

In these constructions, the article alone is very often enough (**el lunes**), as the context usually makes it clear whether *next* or *last* is meant.

The preposition **en** is possible with the days of the week:

| | |
|---|---|
| Yo no trabajo **en sábado**. | *I don't work on Saturdays.* |

But **los sábados** would be more common in the above example. **En** is rarely used when demonstratives or articles (**este, ese, aquel, un**, etc.) precede:

| | |
|---|---|
| Yo no trabajo **este sábado**. | *I'm not working this Saturday.* |

Note that **en** usually requires singular nouns when no demonstratives or articles are used (e.g., **en sábados** is highly unusual), but it is very common with the plural noun **días**.

| | |
|---|---|
| La farmacia está abierta **en** (o: **los**) **días festivos**. | *The pharmacy is open on holidays.* |

With the verb **estar**, the preposition **a** is needed to refer to a specific day of the week:

| | |
|---|---|
| ¿**A** qué día estamos? | *What day is it?* |
| Estamos **a** viernes. | *It's Friday.* |

The preposition **a** is also used in headings of letters or other documents to refer to the day on which the text was written:

| | |
|---|---|
| En Madrid, **a** dos de enero de 2008 | *Madrid, January 2, 2008* |

In more informal language, the prepositions **en** and **a** are usually omitted:

Madrid, dos de enero de 2008

Note that in Spanish dates, both the month and the year are preceded by **de**. To refer to a day of a month, use the definite article **el** before the number (without a preposition):

Ellos estarán con nosotros **el seis de mayo**.     *They will be with us on May 6.*
Los exámenes son **el veinticinco de junio**.     *The exams are on June 25.*

With nouns like **día** (*day*), **semana** (*week*), **mes** (*month*), and, in general, all words that refer to periods of time (including words such as **segundo**, **momento**, etc.), **en** is used:

Lo haré **en un segundo**.     *I'll do it in a second.*
Estaré con vosotros **en un minuto**.     *I'll be with you in a minute.*
Ella nació **en enero**.     *She was born in January.*
Ocurrió **en Navidad**.     *It happened at Christmas.*

**Estar** + **a** is used with the days of the week, but **en** must be used with the time words listed above. Compare:

Estamos **a** viernes.     *It's Friday.*
Estamos **en** enero.     *It's January.*

When demonstratives and articles are used, the preposition is usually omitted:

Terminaremos **este mes**.     *We will finish this month.*
Lo haré **un día de éstos**.     *I'll do it one of these days.*
**Aquella semana** tuve muchos problemas.     *I had a lot of problems that week.*

Sometimes, in literary writing or for emphasis, the preposition is included, especially with indefinite articles and when the time word is qualified by another word (sometimes preceded by the preposition **de**):

Todo sucedió **en un día muy oscuro**.     *It all happened on a very dark day.*
**En esos meses de invierno** no trabajamos.     *In those winter months we don't work.*

The preposition **en** is always omitted in constructions of the type **el mes que viene** or **la semana pasada**.

In narration, *the next/following* + time word translates as **a/al** + time word + **siguiente** (the adjective **siguiente** can also precede the time word):

**Al día siguiente** estuve enfermo.     *I was sick the following day.*
**A la siguiente semana** ella se casó.     *She got married the next week.*

In this case, the preposition **a** can't be omitted.

With the relative pronoun **que**, omission of the preposition **en** in time clauses is optional:

| el año **en el que** nací/el año **en que** nací/el año **que** nací | *the year that I was born* |
| la semana **en la que** vine/la semana **en que** vine/la semana **que** vine | *the week that I came* |

In sentences with relative pronouns it is even possible to put the preposition **en** at the beginning of the sentence (before the time word). In this case the preposition **en** refers to the whole of the period indicated by the time word:

| **En la semana que** estuve aquí... | *In/During the week that I was here . . .* |

In this type of construction there may be differences of meaning or intention. The clause **En el año que estuve aquí...** tells us clearly that the speaker was here for a year, but the clause **El año que estuve aquí...** doesn't necessarily mean this; maybe the speaker was here for a short visit *in the course of* that year. In other words, omission of the preposition gives the sentence a wider range of meaning. The context will probably make the meaning clear. Two simple examples will help clarify this:

| La semana que estuve aquí estuvo llena de sorpresas. | *The week that (or: in which) I was here was full of surprises.* |
| En la semana que estuve aquí tuve dos accidentes. | *In the week that I was here I had two accidents.* |

In the first example above **la semana** is the subject; in the second example **en la semana** is a time complement, a period during which something happened. (In the second example the preposition **en** can also be omitted.)

With the words **segundo**, **minuto**, **instante**, and so on, the preposition **en** must *not* be used to convey the English *for*:

| Estaré contigo **en** un minuto. | *I'll be with you **in** a minute.* |
| Sólo la vi un minuto. | *I only saw her **for** a minute.* |
| Estuvimos allí un momento/instante. | *We were there **for** a moment.* |

This rule is also applicable to other time words:

| Lo terminaré **en** dos horas. | *I'll finish it **in** two hours' time.* |
| Tuve que prepararlo **en** tres meses. | *I had to prepare it **in** three months.* |

**En** cannot be omitted in the above examples.

| Lo necesito dos horas. | *I need it **for** two hours.* |
| Tuve que quedarme allí tres meses. | *I had to stay there **for** three months.* |

**En** cannot be used above.

Don't use the preposition **sobre** to translate *on* in time expressions such as *on this occasion*, which must be translated as **en esta ocasión**. The Spanish preposition **sobre**, when used with time words, means *about/approximately*:

Nos veremos **sobre la una**.      *We'll meet at about one o'clock.*

In general, it is incorrect to omit prepositions in Spanish with time expressions; only **en** can be omitted in the time clauses already covered.

With parts of the day and other time words, the preposition **a** is frequent, but there are other possibilities:

| | |
|---|---|
| a la mañana | *in the morning* |
| a la tarde | *in the afternoon* |
| a la noche | *in the evening/at night* |
| al alba | *at dawn* |
| al amanecer | *at sunrise* |
| al anochecer | *at sunset* |

With the words **mañana**, **tarde**, and **noche**, the preposition **a** usually refers to the *next* morning, afternoon, or night, while **por** has a wider usage:

| | |
|---|---|
| Ella nunca viene **por la tarde**. | *She never comes in the afternoon.* |
| Les veremos **a/por la tarde**. | *We'll see them in the afternoon.* |
| | *(i.e., this or that afternoon)* |

**Por la noche** can usually be replaced by **de noche** (*in the evening/at night/by night*):

| | |
|---|---|
| Nunca estudio **de noche** (o: **por la noche**). | *I never study in the evening (or: at night).* |
| Llegaremos mañana **por la noche** (o: **de noche**). | *We will arrive tomorrow evening (or: night).* |

It is possible, and even common, to say **mañana noche** (without the preposition), but this can't be done with other parts of the day.

When another time phrase appears before **mañana**, **tarde**, or **noche**, the preposition **de** is used, *not* **por**:

| | |
|---|---|
| a las once **de la mañana** | *at eleven o'clock in the morning* |
| Ella me despertó en mitad **de la noche**. | *She woke me up in the middle of the night.* |

The time between midnight and sunrise is called **la madrugada**. With the word **madrugada** you can use both **de** and **por la**:

| | |
|---|---|
| Nunca trabajo **de madrugada** (o: **por la madrugada**). | *I never work late at night.* |

When a specific event is narrated, you can use the preposition **en** and definite articles or no preposition at all; this is a case where *on* is used in English:

| | |
|---|---|
| **En la mañana** (o: **La mañana**) del 8 de abril recibimos importantes noticias. | *On the morning of April 8 we got important news.* |

In this type of sentence, when demonstrative adjectives are used (generally for emphasis) the preposition is omitted in Spanish:

| | |
|---|---|
| **Esa mañana** del 8 de abril recibí... | *On that morning of April 8 I received . . .* |

With *tomorrow* + the words *morning*, *afternoon*, and *evening/night*, no preposition is used. In Spanish, **por** is used:

| | |
|---|---|
| Nos veremos mañana **por la mañana**. | *We'll see each other tomorrow morning.* |

This is also applicable to the combination day of the week + *morning/afternoon/evening*:

| | |
|---|---|
| el lunes **por la mañana** | *on Monday morning* |
| el viernes **por la noche** | *on Friday evening* |

English constructions of the type *tomorrow's meeting* (genitive + noun) must be translated using the construction noun + **de** + time word:

| | |
|---|---|
| **La clase de mañana** ha sido aplazada. | *Tomorrow's class has been put off.* |
| **El periódico de hoy** no dice nada. | *Today's paper doesn't say anything.* |

In saying what time something happens, the English preposition *at* translates as **a**:

| | |
|---|---|
| Ellos vienen **a las ocho**. | *They are coming at eight.* |
| Las tiendas abren **a las diez**. | *The shops open at ten.* |

In questions of the type *What time . . . ?*, the question is always preceded by the preposition **a** when it refers to the start of an action:

| | |
|---|---|
| **¿A qué hora** empieza la película? | *What time does the film start?* |
| **¿A qué hora** vas a venir? | *What time are you going to come?* |

The word **hora** means both *time* and *hour*. It requires the preposition **a** when it means a point in time (**a qué hora...** ) and the preposition **en** when it refers to a period of time (**en dos horas**).

The grammatical implications already covered with regard to the relative pronoun **que** apply here as well:

**La hora a la que** ella vino era muy extraña.   *The time at which she came was very strange.*

**A la hora que** ella vino estábamos cenando.   *At the time she came we were having dinner.*

When referring to mealtimes, the preposition **en** is used with the nouns **desayuno** (*breakfast*), **almuerzo** (*lunch*), **comida** (*dinner*), and **cena** (*dinner, supper*):

| | |
|---|---|
| **en** el desayuno | *at breakfast* |
| **en** la cena | *at dinner* |

Reference to level, points on a scale, measures, figures, and words that can be represented by figures (e.g., *midday, twelve o'clock, 12:00*) usually require the preposition **a**:

| | |
|---|---|
| a mediodía | *at midday, noon* |
| a las dos | *at two o'clock* |
| a 2.000 pies | *at 2,000 feet* |
| a esa distancia | *at that distance* |
| a esta altura | *at this height* |
| al principio | *at/in the beginning* |
| al final | *at/in the end* |
| a dos dólares | *at two dollars* |
| a esa edad | *at that age* |

English questions with *how* + adjective are usually translated by the construction **qué** + noun. This interrogative construction is always preceded by the preposition **a** when the question refers to position/location/level:

| | |
|---|---|
| ¿**A qué altura** está volando el avión? | *How high is the plane flying?* |
| ¿**A qué distancia** está tu colegio? | *How far is your school?* |
| ¿**A qué profundidad** está el submarino? | *How deep is the submarine?* |

The preposition **a** is *not* used when the question asks about physical description:

| | |
|---|---|
| ¿**Qué altura** tiene esa montaña? | *How high is that mountain?* |
| ¿**Qué profundidad** tiene el lago? | *How deep is the lake?* |

With relative pronouns there may be differences in use of prepositions:

**La distancia a la que** estamos es enorme.   *The distance at which we are is huge.*

**A la distancia que** estamos no vemos.   *At this distance (i.e., the distance we are at) we can't see.*

In the first example above the subject is **la distancia**; subjects can't be preceded by prepositions. In the second example, **la distancia** is a complement, so **a** is used in the same way that *at* is used in English.

To express *at* in *to be good/bad at (something)* requires **en**:

Ella es muy buena **en inglés**.        *She is very good at English.*

No preposition is required when a verb form (present participle) follows:

Ella es muy buena **conduciendo**.        *She is very good at driving.*

The preposition *in*, when referring to school subjects, conversations, films, and so on, translates as **en**:

Tengo un sobresaliente **en español**.     *I have an A in Spanish.*
Ellos no tomaron parte **en la carrera**.     *They didn't take part in the race.*
Ella estaba muy guapa **en esa foto**.     *She was very beautiful in that photo.*

The English preposition *on* is often used with the same meaning as *about* to refer to subjects or topics (especially those that are serious or academic). In Spanish, **de** or **sobre** must be used:

Tengo un libro **de/sobre economía**.     *I have a book on economics.*

The English construction *on/in* + gerund (present participle) translates as **al** + infinitive:

**Al llegar** les vi.        ***On/Upon arriving*** *I saw them.*

**Dentro de** translates as *in* when it is followed by numbers and time words:

Vendré **dentro de** dos días.        *I'll come back in two days' time.*

**EJERCICIO**
**10·1**

*Fill in the blanks with a suitable preposition.*

1. _____ veces pienso que no me quieres.

2. El barril de petróleo está _____ más de 40 dólares.

3. ¿_____ qué precio se está vendiendo el oro?

4. El accidente fue _____ las proximidades de la oficina de tu padre.

5. Lo terminaré todo _____ un par de días.

6. Creo que el cuadro quedará mejor _____ metro y medio del suelo.

7. _____ la mañana siguiente nos tuvimos que marchar.

8. Papá, _____ tu edad no deberías hacer esas cosas.

9. La granja está _____ mitad del valle.

10. _____ el fondo sí creo en Dios.

EJERCICIO
10·2

*Find and correct any mistakes.*

1. Estamos a media hora de camino.

2. Mi padre es muy bueno en contando historias.

3. Nos reuniremos todos a la Navidad.

4. ¿Qué altura está volando el avión?

5. El restaurante está en unos doscientos metros de la orilla.

6. Me enamoré una soleada y hermosa mañana de primavera.

7. El protagonista muere al final.

8. Me lo pasé muy bien a la boda de Miguel.

9. Te lo contaré todo a la cena.

10. Había un montón de periódicos en el suelo.

*Underline the correct choice. In some cases both answers are possible. A hyphen indicates that no word is necessary.*

1. Me encanta quedarme **a/en** casa **en/los** días de lluvia y mirar por los cristales.

2. No suelo estar **a/en** la oficina **en/los** domingos **en/por** la mañana.

3. Los actos violentos se desataron **en/de** madrugada, aproximadamente **en/a** las tres.

4. Les vi **en/por** la tarde, **el/al** salir del cine.

5. Mañana **en/por** la tarde tengo que esperarles **en/a** la salida de la estación.

6. Mis hijos siempre me visitan **en/los** días de fiesta, pero **en/-** éste próximo no van a poder venir.

7. Marta no sabe **en/-** qué día nació su abuela, pero sí sabe que fue **a/en** mayo.

8. Cenaremos **a/en** Casa Roberto, **en/-** donde ponen unas pizzas enormes.

9. He estado **en el/al** dentista, pero no me han hecho nada **a/en** la boca.

10. Marta estaba sentada **en/a** la derecha de Juan, **en/a** la parte trasera del auditorio.

# Problematic prepositions II

This unit covers the prepositions *above, across, below, down, into, off, onto, out of, over, through, to, toward, under,* and *up.* The most logical way to deal with these prepositions is to divide them into two groups: prepositions that are related to movement and those that are related to position and other contexts.

## Movement

Prepositions play a very important role in expressing movement. Although Spanish has different verbs for different types of movement, the use of prepositions can determine the direction and, in many cases, hidden nuances connected with movement.

### To and *toward*

The preposition **a** is probably the most important preposition commonly translated as *to/toward.* When a Spanish verb expresses movement or direction *toward* a certain point, the preposition **a** must be used:

| | |
|---|---|
| Pedro **llegó a** su casa a las diez. | *Pedro arrived at his house at ten.* |
| Ellos **llegaron a** París de noche. | *They arrived in Paris at night.* |
| Juan **se fue a** la casa de su abuela. | *Juan went to his grandmother's house.* |
| Ella **se marchó a** Bélgica. | *She left for Belgium.* |
| **Tiré** la pelota **al** río. | *I threw the ball into the river.* |
| Ella **apuntó a** su marido con un arma. | *She pointed at her husband with a weapon.* |

Note that in the English equivalents there are many different prepositions (*arrived at/in, left for,* etc.).

The preposition **hacia** (*toward*) is used much less frequently than **a**. In many cases **a** and **hacia** are interchangeable, but whenever speakers focus their attention on the movement itself, they usually prefer **hacia**. In addition to this, there are verbs that "sound better" with **hacia** (e.g., **caminar**):

| | |
|---|---|
| **Caminé hacia** el bosque. | *I walked to/toward the forest.* |
| El avión **está volando hacia** su objetivo. | *The plane is flying toward its target.* |

With pronouns, **hacia** is preferred:

| | |
|---|---|
| Vienen **hacia nosotros**. | *They are coming to/toward us.* |
| Fui **hacia ellos**. | *I went up to them. (Or: I went toward them.)* |

A simple rule of thumb: limit the use of **hacia** to those cases in which *toward* would be used in English.

Besides **a** and **hacia**, the preposition **para** is often used to refer to movement toward a place:

| | |
|---|---|
| Me fui **para/a/hacia** mi casa. | *I went to my house.* |
| Mañana **salgo para/hacia** Nueva York. | *I am leaving for New York tomorrow.* |
| **Sal para** fuera/afuera. (O: Sal fuera/afuera.) | *Get out./Go out./Come out.* |
| **Tira para/a/hacia** la derecha. | *Go to the right.* |

## Into, onto, out of, and off

In English, many kinds of movement are expressed by means of a verb that conveys the idea of movement (*go, come, walk, ride, drive,* etc.) and a preposition or an adverb. It is even possible to use the verb *to get* with prepositions that express movement colloquially (*he got out of the room, she got into town,* etc.). In Spanish, different types of movement require different verbs and prepositions. Here are some examples:

*Put* + noun/pronoun + *in(to)* translates as **meter/poner** + noun/pronoun + **en** or **dentro de**:

| | |
|---|---|
| Ella **metió** la carne **en** el frigorífico. | *She put the meat into the fridge.* |

The prepositions **en** and **de** are not used when the place is not mentioned. This applies to the following combinations as well.

*Take* + noun/pronoun + *out (of)* translates as **sacar** + noun/pronoun (+ **de**):

| | |
|---|---|
| **Saqué** el dinero **de** la caja. | *I took the money out of the box.* |
| Ellos **sacaron** los libros **de** la caja. | *They took the books out of the box.* |

*Take* + noun/pronoun + *off* translates as **quitar** + noun/pronoun + **de**:

| | |
|---|---|
| **Quita** todos esos libros **de** la mesa. | *Take all those books off the table.* |

The combination *come/go/get* + *in(to)* translates as **entrar** + **en**, no matter where the speaker is situated. The preposition **en** is omitted when the place is not mentioned:

| | |
|---|---|
| No debes **entrar en** esa habitación. | *You mustn't go into that room.* |
| Entra, por favor. | *Come/Go/Get in, please.* |

In this context the verb **pasar** is equally acceptable, but it is usually used without mentioning the place (and without a preposition):

| | |
|---|---|
| Pasa, por favor. | *Come/Go/Get in, please.* |

When the place is mentioned, the verb **pasar** takes the preposition **a**:

| | |
|---|---|
| Ella **pasó a** la habitación. | *She went/came into the room.* |

The preposition **a** is not used when **pasar** is followed by the adverb **adentro** or the preposition **dentro de**. It is also possible and even common to use **para** and **hacia** with these words:

| | |
|---|---|
| Pasa dentro/adentro. | *Come in/Get in. (adverbial use)* |
| Pasa dentro (o: para dentro) de la clase. | *Come inside the classroom.* |

The English verb *to enter* translates as **entrar**. The preposition **en** is needed when the place entered is mentioned:

| | |
|---|---|
| **Entraron en** la iglesia. | *They entered the church.* |

It is possible to use verbs like **ir** (*go*), **venir** (*come*), **caminar** (*walk*), and so on together with **dentro de/hacia dentro de/al interior de** (or similar expressions):

| | |
|---|---|
| Fueron hacia el interior de la casa. | *They went into the house.* |

The combination *come/go/get* + *out (of)* translates as **salir** (+ **de**):

| | |
|---|---|
| Juan **salió de** la casa. | *Juan came/went/got out of the house.* |
| **¡Sal!** | *Come/Go/Get out!* |

In this context, the English verb *to leave* is usually translated as **salir** (**de**) or **marcharse** (**de**):

| | |
|---|---|
| Tienes que **salir de** ese lugar. | *You have to leave that place.* |
| María **se marchó de** la fiesta. | *María left the party.* |

Similarly to what happens with *into*, you can translate *out of* as **afuera de/hacia fuera de** (or similar expressions) together with verbs that imply movement:

| | |
|---|---|
| Caminemos hacia fuera de la casa. | *Let's walk out of the house.* |

*Get + into/onto* followed by the name of a vehicle translates as **montarse (en)** or **subirse (a)**:

| | |
|---|---|
| Me monté en el auto. (O: Me subí al auto.) | *I got into the car.* |
| Me monté en la moto. (O: Me subí a la moto.) | *I got onto the motorcycle.* |

*Get + out (of)/off* followed by the name of a vehicle translates as **bajarse (de)**:

| | |
|---|---|
| Ella se bajó del auto. | *She got out of the car.* |
| Ella se bajó de la bici. | *She got off the bike.* |

Remember that **del** is the contraction of **de + el**. *Out of* can also be translated as **fuera (de)** with any verb that implies movement.

The verbs **subirse (a)** and **bajarse (de)** are also used to express movement related to surface (*onto/off/down from*):

| | |
|---|---|
| ¡Bájate de la mesa! | *Get off the table!* |
| Ellos se bajaron del tejado. | *They came down from the roof.* |
| El perro se subió a la mesa. | *The dog got onto the table.* |

When the movement is connected with small interiors (boxes, bags, etc.), **meterse (en)** and **salir(se) (de)** are used:

| | |
|---|---|
| El gato se metió en la caja. | *The cat got into the box.* |
| El ratón (se) salió de la bolsa. | *The mouse got out of the bag.* |

**Meterse en** is very often used in casual conversation instead of **entrar (en)**:

| | |
|---|---|
| Me metí en el cuarto de baño. | *I went into the bathroom.* |
| Ella se metió en la biblioteca. | *She went into the library.* |

**Meterse (en)**, **entrar (en)**, and **salir(se) (de)** can even be used to translate *to get into/onto/out of/off* vehicles:

| | |
|---|---|
| Me metí en el auto. | *I got into the car.* |
| Ella (se) salió del taxi. | *She got out of the taxi.* |

*Get + to* usually translates as **llegar a**:

| | |
|---|---|
| Ellos llegaron a la casa. | *They got to the house.* |

# Across, over, and through

*Across* and *over* translate as **por** when the movement is somehow connected with the idea of wandering or walking inside an area:

| | |
|---|---|
| Él deambulaba **por los campos**. | *He was wandering across/over the fields.* |
| Él caminaba **por la habitación**. | *He was walking across the room.* |

**Por** also indicates the way that has to be followed to get somewhere:

| | |
|---|---|
| Venga **por aquí**, por favor. | *Come over here, please.* |

When the movement goes from one side of a surface to the other, the verbs **atravesar** (*go/get across*) and **cruzar** (*cross*) are used without a preposition:

| | |
|---|---|
| Ellos atravesaron el desierto. | *They went across the desert.* |
| (O: Ellos cruzaron el desierto.) | |

It is also possible to use verbs like **caminar**, **ir**, and so on and the construction **a través de** (*across/over/through*):

| | |
|---|---|
| Ellos caminaron a través del desierto. | *They walked across the desert.* |

The only difference in meaning is that **caminar/ir a través de** doesn't indicate whether the action was completed or not. In translating that *they walked across the desert and reached the other side*, the verbs **atravesar** and **cruzar** are preferable.

Verbs such as *walk* or *run* are used in English in order to explain how the movement took place. The verb **atravesar** and a gerund are often used in Spanish:

| | |
|---|---|
| Ellos atravesaron el desierto **andando/ caminando**. | *They walked across the desert.* |

It is not correct to use **atravesar** with **a través de**, as they imply practically the same thing. In English, *across* and *over* are both used to indicate movement on or to the other side of something that is long and thin (river, road, etc.). In Spanish, the preposition depends on the verb used. With **ir**, **caminar**, **pasar**, and **saltar**, the combinations **al otro lado de** or **hacia el otro lado de** (*at/on/to/toward the other side of*) are normally used:

| | |
|---|---|
| Fuimos **al otro** (o: **hacia el otro**) **lado** de la calle. | *We walked across the street.* |
| Ella no pudo saltar **al otro** (o: **hacia el otro**) **lado** del arroyo. | *She couldn't jump over/across the stream.* |

**Saltar** can be used without a preposition: **Ella no pudo saltar el arroyo.**

If you use the verbs **atravesar** or **cruzar**, no prepositions are required:

| | |
|---|---|
| Atravesamos/Cruzamos la calle. | *We walked across the street.* |
| Tendremos que atravesar/cruzar la frontera. | *We will have to get over/across the border.* |

The verbs **atravesar** and **cruzar** can be used with **arroyo** (*stream*), **río** (*river*), and so on, but then the idea of being in/on the water is conveyed, whereas in English, *over* generally indicates a movement on or above something:

| | |
|---|---|
| Conseguí cruzar/atravesar el río. | *I succeeded in getting across the river. (by swimming or by boat)* |

The preposition **por** can be used with the noun **agua** to indicate that the movement takes place in or on water, not above. **Ellos cruzaron por el agua** implies that they got to the other side, but by swimming, walking, or in a boat.

**A través de** and the verb **atravesar** can also be used for movement *through* a three-dimensional space:

| | |
|---|---|
| Atravesamos el bosque. (O: Fuimos a través del bosque.) | *We went through the forest.* |

*Over* is usually not translated when expressing a movement from one side to the other of something high, especially with the verbs **saltar**, **escalar** (*climb*), **pasar**, and **atravesar**:

| | |
|---|---|
| El perro saltó la mesa. | *The dog jumped over the table.* |
| Escalé la valla. | *I climbed over the fence.* |

Even the verb **cruzar** (without a preposition), which is normally connected with the idea of crossing, is often used to talk about movements over something high:

| | |
|---|---|
| El avión cruzó/atravesó/pasó los Alpes. | *The plane flew over the Alps.* |

**Al otro lado de** or **hacia el otro lado de** can accompany the verbs **saltar** and **pasar**, especially when the context is not very clear:

| | |
|---|---|
| Pasé al otro lado de la valla. | *I got/went/climbed over the fence.* |

Instead of the noun **lado** (*side*), you can use **parte** (*part, side*). When expressing movement, these nouns can also be accompanied by the preposition **hacia**. The preposition **por** is not possible to express movement to the other side of something, but it is possible when the speaker indicates the place where the movement started. **Salté por la valla** means that I jumped where the fence was situated (not somewhere else).

*Over* and *across* can also be translated by **sobre** for movements on or above the surface of something; however, **sobre** doesn't necessarily indicate movement from one side to the other:

| | |
|---|---|
| La tormenta se movía sobre Inglaterra. | *The storm was moving over England.* |
| El avión voló sobre los Alpes. | *The plane flew over the Alps.* |

## *Up* and *down*

Combinations of verbs of movement in English and the preposition *up* are usually translated using **subir**, but it is possible to use the construction verb of movement + noun + **arriba**:

| | |
|---|---|
| Subí la montaña. | *I went/climbed up the mountain.* |
| Fui montaña arriba. | *I went/climbed up the mountain.* |

In the second example, it is not clear whether the subject reached the top of the mountain or not. In the first example it is clear that he or she did, since the preterit of the verb **subir** refers to completed actions. The second example indicates only the direction, not the final destination, despite the use of the preterit. To indicate that the final destination was reached, the prepositions **hasta** (*as far as*) or **a** and expressions like **lo alto de** (*the top of*) or **la parte superior de** (*the top of*) are used:

| | |
|---|---|
| Fui hasta lo alto de la montaña. | *I went up (and reached the top of) the mountain.* |

**Subir** can also be used with these expressions for emphasis.

Since **subir** doesn't say how an action takes place, you will have to add gerunds (present participles) or adverbial phrases to indicate that the movement takes place by driving, walking, and so on:

| | |
|---|---|
| Subí la calle **en coche**. | *I drove up the street.* |
| Subieron el río **nadando**. | *They swam up the river.* |

**En coche** means *by car* and **nadando** means *swimming*. If these words were not added, you would not know how the action was performed. Another possibility is to use the same verbs as in English and the construction noun + **arriba**:

| | |
|---|---|
| Conduje calle arriba. | *I drove up the street.* |
| Nadaron río arriba. | *They swam up the river.* |

When **subir** acts as a transitive verb (i.e., followed by a direct object), it can *never* be replaced by the above constructions:

| | |
|---|---|
| **Subí los libros** a mi habitación. | *I took the books up to my room.* |

*Down* usually translates as **abajo**, which follows nouns:

| | |
|---|---|
| calle abajo | *down the street* |
| río abajo | *down the river* |

The combination of *down* and verbs that imply movement (e.g., *come/go/walk down*) becomes **bajar**, although **ir/venir** (and other verbs that imply movement) + noun + **abajo** is a possible alternative:

| | |
|---|---|
| Ellos bajaron la calle. | *They went down the street.* |
| Ellos fueron/caminaron calle abajo. | *They went/walked down the street.* |

The second example offers the same problem as *up*. It doesn't say whether the subject reached his or her destination or not. In such cases it is better to use **hasta** or **a** followed by **el fondo de** (*the bottom of*), **la parte inferior de** (*the bottom of*), and similar expressions:

| | |
|---|---|
| Fui hasta el fondo de la calle. | *I went down (and reached the bottom of) the street.* |

**Bajar** doesn't say how the action is done. This means that in translating *to drive down the hill* (**bajar la colina**), the verb **bajar** says nothing about driving. To address this problem, you can add **en coche** (*by car*) or the gerund **conduciendo** (*driving*).

English speakers often use *down* with the noun *street* without considering whether the street has different levels or not. In such cases the best translation for *down (the street)* is **por** (**la calle**) since **por** is a more general word for location.

When **bajar** is followed by a direct object, it means *to take/get/let down*:

| | |
|---|---|
| **Bajé las sillas** de mi habitación. | *I took the chairs down from my room.* |

# Position and location

The English prepositions that are covered in this section are often translated by complex constructions. These constructions are not prepositions but sequences with a prepositional function.

## Over, above, and below

When level is meant, *over* and *above* are translated as **sobre** and as **por encima de**. With figures and words that can be represented by figures (level, height, etc.), **sobre** is preferred:

| | |
|---|---|
| El agua nos llegaba **sobre/por encima de** las rodillas. | *The water came up above/over our knees.* |
| Pusieron una bolsa de plástico **por encima del** cuerpo. | *They put a plastic bag over the body.* |
| La temperatura es de diez grados **sobre** cero. | *The temperature is ten degrees above zero.* |
| El pueblo está a mil metros **sobre** el nivel del mar. | *The town is at one thousand meters above sea level.* |
| El helicóptero está volando **sobre/por encima de** la ciudad. | *The helicopter is flying over/above the town.* |

The preposition **por** in **por encima de** can be left out in the examples above. Its presence in a prepositional construction is often redundant:

| | |
|---|---|
| La lámpara está **sobre/encima de** nuestras cabezas. | *The lamp is over/above our heads.* |
| Había extrañas nubes **sobre/encima de** la ciudad. | *There were strange clouds over/above the city.* |

In English, *over* is related to the idea of covering and *above* is related to level on a vertical scale. The Spanish preposition **sobre** and the construction (**por**) **encima de** can relate to both, but the speaker usually has the idea of covering in mind. If you want to express something like *The cloud is above the house but not over it,* don't use either one. In this case it is much better to refer to height with the verb **estar** (**La nube está más alta que la casa, pero no está encima**).

In the preceding examples, **sobre** and (**por**) **encima de** don't imply physical contact, but they can do so in other contexts. **Encima de** then translates as *on, on top of,* and *at the top of:*

| | |
|---|---|
| Los platos están **sobre/encima de** la mesa. | *The plates are on the table.* |
| Las mantas están **sobre/encima del** armario. | *The blankets are on top of the wardrobe.* |

In these sentences, **encima de** can be replaced by **en lo alto de**:

| | |
|---|---|
| Los he puesto **en lo alto del** armario (o: **encima del** armario/**sobre** el armario). | *I have put them on top of the wardrobe.* |

When no place of reference is mentioned, the preposition **de** is left out (adverbial function):

| | |
|---|---|
| Los puse **encima**. | *I put them on top (of it).* |
| Lo dejé **en lo alto**. | *I left it on top (of it).* |

*Over* and *across* translate as **al otro lado de** or **en la otra parte de** when they mean *at the other side of*:

> Hay un pueblo **al otro lado de** las colinas.   *There is a town over the hills.*

*All over* translates as **por todo**:

> por todo el mundo                                  *all over the world*

The preposition *over* can be used in English with meals/food/drink. In this case its translation is **durante** or **en**:

> Tuvimos una agradable charla **durante/**         *We had a nice chat over lunch.*
>   **en** el almuerzo.

*Over* is translated as **en** + infinitive in sentences of the type *He doesn't take long over lunch*: **Él no tarda mucho en almorzar.** In this construction the verb *take* is translated using **tardar**; the noun *lunch* becomes a verb (**almorzar**).

*Over* can mean *more than* or *higher than*. Its translation is **más de** (for figures) or (**por**) **encima de** (for situation/location):

> Hay **más de** 5.000 personas aquí.               *There are over 5,000 people here.*
> Nos llegaba **por encima de** las rodillas.        *It came up over our knees.*

You can also use **más arriba de** in the second example.

**Arriba** (adverb) is used to refer to location on a higher floor or to refer to a place situated somewhere else at a higher level. **Arriba** isn't used with **de** and nouns or pronouns, except in the construction **más arriba de**:

> Ellos viven **encima de nosotros.**               *They live above us. (in the same building,*
>   (O: Ellos viven **arriba**.)                     *for example)*

**Ellos están arriba** can mean *They are upstairs*, or it can mean that they are in a known place that is situated at a higher level with regard to the speaker. The context and the situation will make it clear.

Both *over* and *above* can mean *higher in rank*. In this case, **por encima de** is used:

> Ella está por encima de él.                        *She is over him.*

To say *over* as in *a bridge over a river*, the prepositions **sobre** and **en** are used:

> un puente sobre el Támesis                         *a bridge over the Thames*

*Above the bridge* is translated by **corriente arriba** (*upstream*) or **río arriba** (*up the river*).

*Below* translates as **bajo** when it refers to level and figures connected to level:

| | |
|---|---|
| La temperatura ahora es de diez grados **bajo cero**. | *The temperature now is ten degrees below zero.* |
| Partes de Holanda están **bajo el nivel del mar**. | *Parts of Holland are below sea level.* |

In other contexts, speakers prefer (**por**) **debajo de** for *below*, although **bajo** is equally correct in most cases, except with pronouns (e.g., **bajo él** isn't good Spanish). The preposition **por** can usually be left out:

| | |
|---|---|
| Ellos viven **debajo de** nosotros. | *They live below us.* |

In the above example, we might live, for instance, on the third floor and they live on the second. If they lived farther down the street on a lower level (a steep street), Spanish speakers would never use **por debajo de** or **bajo**. In such a case they would say **más abajo de**. **Ellos viven debajo de nosotros** can also be **Ellos viven abajo**, without mentioning **nosotros**.

## *Up* and *down*

*Up* translates as **en lo alto de/en la parte superior de/en la parte de arriba de**, and so on when position/location is meant:

| | |
|---|---|
| Estaban **en lo alto de** la colina. | *They were up the hill.* |

*Down* corresponds to **en lo hondo de/en** (or: **al**) **fondo de/en la parte de abajo de/en la parte inferior de**, and so on when it indicates position/location:

| | |
|---|---|
| Están **al fondo de** la colina. | *They are down the hill.* |

## *Under*

*Under* usually translates as **debajo** (**de**):

| | |
|---|---|
| El gato está **debajo de** la mesa. | *The cat is under the table.* |
| Ella puso la carta **debajo de** la almohada. | *She put the letter under the pillow.* |

**Bajo** can also be used in these examples.

Very often **por debajo de** is an alternative, especially when verbs indicating movement are used:

| | |
|---|---|
| Ellos estaban nadando **por debajo del** agua (o: ... **bajo** el agua). | *They were swimming underwater.* |

The preposition **por** can usually be omitted.

When *below* and *under* are used to refer to seniority, Spanish speakers usually prefer **por debajo de**. The noun **responsabilidad** (*responsibility*) is used with **bajo**:

> Ellos están **por debajo** de mí.   *They are under me.*
> Lo haré **bajo mi responsabilidad**.   *I'll do it and take the responsibility.*

*Beneath* usually translates as **(por) debajo de**, to which very often possessive adjective + **nivel/clase** (or similar noun) is added:

> Ella se casó **por debajo de** su nivel/clase.   *She married beneath her station/class.*

**EJERCICIO**
**11·1**

*Fill in the blanks with a suitable preposition or prepositional expression. If no preposition is needed, mark the blank with a hyphen. For many items, there is more than one possible answer.*

1. La multitud se dirigía _____ la comisaría de policía.

2. Los invitados llegaron muy temprano _____ la recepción.

3. Me fui _____ afuera sin ponerme el abrigo.

4. Me lastimé el brazo al saltar _____ el seto del jardín.

5. Hace muchísimo frío. La temperatura es de doce grados _____ cero.

6. El puente que van a construir _____ ese río mide más de cien metros de longitud.

7. Los pobres tuvieron que caminar _____ el desierto sin agua ni comida.

8. Los tuve que poner _____ del aparador para que los niños no los alcanzaran.

9. Relacionarme con gente así está _____ mi clase, y no pienso rebajarme.

10. He viajado _____ todo el mundo.

*Find and correct any mistakes.*

1. Siempre voy allí por coche.

2. La chica que vive encima de mi piso es azafata.

3. Paco está bajo ella en la oficina. Ella es su jefa.

4. Podremos discutir las condiciones del contrato encima del almuerzo.

5. Estuve dando un paseo por el parque.

6. Ven para acá y échame una mano con esto.

7. Atravesamos a través de un boquecillo que hay en las afueras.

8. El dormitorio de Elena está arriba del mío.

9. La chica estuvo montando en bici toda la mañana.

10. Cruzaron el Atlántico en balsa.

*Underline the correct choice. In some cases both answers are possible.*

1. La temperatura es de veinte grados **bajo/debajo de** cero.

2. Los puse **debajo de/bajo** la mesa que hay en el comedor.

3. Los dulces estaban **en lo alto del/encima del** aparador de la cocina.

4. Hay una agencia de viajes **al/el** otro lado de esa calle.

5. Llegaron **en/a** Colombia después de un pésimo viaje.

6. Los enanitos caminaron **al/hacia el** bosque cantando y silbando.

7. Pasa **a/en** mi despacho, por favor.

8. Se marcharon **a/para** casa muy tarde.

9. Estaban todos **dentro de/adentro** la sala de prensa.

10. Mi padre y mi novio discutieron **en/durante** la cena.

# Idiomatic constructions

The expressions in this unit are among the hundreds of idiomatic constructions that are in common use in Spanish. A reasonable knowledge of these constructions provides a very effective tool for making communication much more engaging and interesting. The idioms and examples given are generally not translated, because many of these constructions don't have an immediate, colloquial English translation. English speakers will no doubt come up with their own near equivalents.

**No tener abuela/no hacer falta abuela** is used to refer to people who are confident that they are very good or the best at something and, in general, to people who boast about something:

> Pepe siempre está fanfarroneando de lo bueno que es en matemáticas; desde luego, no le hace falta abuela.

**¡Acabáramos!** expresses that the speaker suddenly understands something:

> ¡Acabáramos! ¡Tú quieres que te preste dinero!

**¡Se acabó!** means that something is considered to be finished or that the speaker is fed up with a situation:

> ¡Se acabó! Ya no hago más deberes hasta mañana.
> ¡No te aguanto más! ¡Se acabó!

**Hacer el agosto** means *to make a lot of money or profit*:

> La policía está multando a todo el mundo. Está claro que el Ayuntamiento está haciendo el agosto.

**Ser agua de borrajas** refers to something without importance:

> Yo creía tener un gran problema, pero al final fue todo agua de borrajas.

**Ahogarse en un vaso de agua** means that the subject is easily depressed by very small problems:

> Sólo tienes que preparar comida para dos personas y ya estás nerviosa. Desde luego, ¡te ahogas en un vaso de agua!

**Hacerse la boca agua** indicates that the subject wants something very much:

> Con tan sólo hablar de los pasteles, se me hace la boca agua.
> Cuando vi la moto, se me hizo la boca agua.

**Ser agua pasada** means that something talked about belongs to the past and nobody should pay attention to it anymore:

> No debes mencionarle eso a Pedro; es agua pasada.

**Buscar una aguja en un pajar** means that looking for somebody/something is extremely difficult:

> Ella me pidió que buscara a su hija en París, pero yo le dije que eso era como buscar una aguja en un pajar.

**Darse aires** expresses that the person referred to considers himself or herself very important. This construction is usually followed by the preposition **de** and a noun:

> Ella se da aires de gran dama, pero en realidad es la hija de un zapatero.

**Estar en el aire** usually refers to somebody/something that is in a very difficult situation or in a situation that depends on something that is not very likely to happen:

> Si no firmamos esos contratos, estamos en el aire.

**Tomar el aire** means *to get some fresh air*, but it can be used to mean *to go for a walk*:

> ¡Estoy harto de estas cuatro paredes! ¡Voy a tomar el aire!

**Estar en el ajo** usually refers to somebody who is involved in something secret or illegal:

> La broma que me gastaron mis amigos sólo fue posible porque mi mujer también estaba en el ajo.

**Caerse el alma (a los pies)** is used to refer to somebody who is suddenly very disappointed or to somebody who suddenly gets very depressed because of something:

> Cuando vi el estado en el que estaba la casa, se me cayó el alma a los pies.

**Como alma que lleva el diablo** means that the action of the verb is done very fast:

Jorge se fue para su casa como alma que lleva el diablo.

**Dar el alta** means *to discharge somebody from medical care*:

Me dieron el alta la semana pasada.

**Dar el alta** is often used in impersonal constructions with third-person plural forms, but it can also have a known subject:

Ella ya está mejor; mañana le dan el alta.
El médico me dio el alta y me mandó a trabajar.

**Darse de alta** means *to join, become a member, register* and it refers to academies, schools, electricity companies, political parties, among others:

Lo primero que tienes que hacer es darte de alta en la compañía eléctrica.

**Allá tú/él** and so on is used to refer to somebody's responsibility for his or her own acts when a bad decision is made or to express disapproval of somebody's behavior:

Veo que sigue usted fumando. Allá usted, pero le advierto que sus pulmones están muy mal.

**Por amor al arte** indicates that the action referred to is done without expecting money for it:

Me tuvieron todo el día pintando y ni siquiera me preguntaron por la factura. Por lo visto creen que yo pinto por amor al arte.

**Estar de buen año** means *to be plump*:

Veo que estás de buen año. Se conoce que te alimentas bien.

**Entrado en años** refers to a person who is becoming older, getting on in years:

Vino a verme una señora entrada en años.

**Quitarse años** means *to lie about one's age*:

No te quites años. Tú estuviste conmigo en el colegio, así que debes de tener cuarenta.

**Estar para el arrastre** indicates that the person referred to is very tired or in very bad physical or mental shape:

¡Estoy para el arrastre! ¡He llevado a mis sobrinos al cine y no veas qué tarde me han dado!

**Estar hecho un asco** indicates that the person referred to is in extremely bad shape. It can also be applied to animals and things:

¡Esta casa está hecha un asco! ¿Por qué no limpias un poco?

**Brillar por su ausencia** implies that the subject referred to is conspicuously absent:

Tus ganas de trabajar, como de costumbre, brillan por su ausencia.

**Cortar/partir el bacalao** means that the people referred to are in charge. It can also mean that somebody is the most important one within a group:

Para conseguir eso tienes que hablar con Ana, que es la que parte el bacalao aquí.

**Darse de baja** means that the subject stops being a member of an organization, drops out. It can also mean that the person referred to doesn't go to work for health reasons:

Aún tienes que darte de baja en la compañía telefónica.
Ayer me di de baja porque me sentía muy mal.

**De balde** is applied to actions that are free (no payment required):

Entré a ver los toros de balde.

**En balde** means *in vain* and is applied to actions that are useless:

Le hice la respiración artificial, pero fue en balde.

**Por barba** means *per person*:

Eso nos va a costar cincuenta dólares por barba.

**Subirse a las barbas de** is applied to somebody who doesn't show respect to his or her superiors:

Voy a tener que despedirle. Se me sube a las barbas cada vez que quiere.

**Meter baza** means *to interrupt (a conversation)*:

No metas baza si no sabes de lo que estamos hablando.

**Dar en el blanco** means *to hit the target*. Figuratively, it means *to guess right*:

Disparé dos veces, pero no di en el blanco.
Al decir que ella robó el dinero has dado en el blanco.

**Quedarse en blanco** is applied to people who have a sudden loss of memory:

Cuando me hicieron la última pregunta me quedé en blanco.

**Pasar la noche en blanco** means *to have a sleepless night*:

> Estoy cansadísimo. He pasado toda la noche en blanco.

**A pedir de boca** implies that something happens in accordance with one's wishes. This expression usually goes with the verb **salir**:

> La fiesta fue un éxito. Todo salió a pedir de boca.

**Abrir boca** refers to having snacks before a big meal in order to increase one's appetite:

> Nos tomamos unas tapas para ir abriendo boca.

**Decir algo con la boca chica** refers to people who say something because circumstances oblige them to, not because they really mean what they say:

> Los políticos dicen muchas cosas con la boca chica.

**Pasarlo bomba** means *to have a great time*:

> Los festejos fueron geniales. Lo pasé bomba.

**A bote pronto** means *very fast* and is used to refer to actions that are done without pausing to think:

> A bote pronto puedo nombrar cinco lugares donde venden eso.

**De bote en bote** means *full* or *packed* and usually refers to crowded places:

> El restaurante estaba de bote en bote.

**Tonto del bote** is applied to people who are really stupid:

> Ese hombre es tonto del bote.

**Buscarse la vida** means *to make a living*. It is usually followed by gerund forms:

> Me busco la vida dando clases de español a extranjeros.

**Calentar la cabeza** refers to the action of trying to convince somebody in an annoying way or talking at length about something, often about something the person spoken to is not interested in:

> Juan se pasó ayer el día calentándome la cabeza con lo que piensa hacer en su casa.

**Estar mal de la cabeza** means *to be mentally unbalanced*:

> Mi profesor de matemáticas está realmente mal de la cabeza.

**Perder la cabeza** means *to lose one's control* or *mind*. It can be used to refer to unusual behavior:

> Antonio perdió la cabeza e invirtió todo su dinero en esa empresa.

**Quitar de la cabeza** means *to discourage (somebody from doing something)*. When followed by the relative pronoun **que**, subjunctive forms are necessary:

> Debes quitarle a tu hijo esa idea de la cabeza.
> Deberíamos quitarle a Jorge de la cabeza que se case con esa mujer.

**A cal y canto** is used with the verb **cerrar** to mean that the place referred to is sealed shut or completely closed:

> La policía cerró la ciudad a cal y canto.

**Dar una de cal y otra de arena** implies that the subject produces both good and bad results:

> Luisa siempre me da una de cal y otra de arena. Unas veces me alaba y otras me pone verde.

**Abrirse camino** expresses that the subject is obtaining good results in life. It usually refers to making money:

> Tienes que estudiar más para poder abrirte camino en la vida.

**Llevar camino de** is used to predict something because of some evidence in the present:

> Esa chica lleva camino de convertirse en una gran bailarina.

**Echar las campanas al vuelo** implies that the subject lets everybody know that something good has happened:

> Todavía no eches las campanas al vuelo, porque aún no he recibido la notificación oficial de mi ascenso.

**Oír campanas y no saber dónde** refers to people who misunderstand something or to people who give their opinion about something without knowing important details:

> ¡Tú has oído campanas y no sabes dónde! ¡Paco y Elena son novios, no hermanos!

**Pasarlas canutas** means *to be in an extremely difficult situation*:

> Esa familia las está pasando canutas; el padre está desempleado, la madre en el hospital y el hijo mayor en la cárcel.

**Costar caro** means *to cost (someone) dearly* (usually because of bad actions or serious mistakes):

> Ayudar a los que participaron en la huelga me costó muy caro; al día siguiente me despidieron a mí también.

**De andar por casa** is applied to all types of things that are simple or basic (not important, beautiful, or fashionable):

> Esta ropa que llevo puesta es de andar por casa.

Figuratively, **de andar por casa** can also be applied to a limited knowledge of something:

> Mi conocimiento de la lengua rusa es de andar por casa.

**Tirar la casa por la ventana** means *to waste money, blow the works*:

> La boda fue de muchísimo lujo. Está claro que tiraron la casa por la ventana.

**Agarrarse a un clavo ardiendo** indicates that the subject does anything so as not to lose something important:

> No me gusta la idea de asociarnos con esa gente, pero hay que agarrarse a un clavo ardiendo para no perder la empresa.

Figuratively, **agarrarse a un clavo ardiendo** refers to people who use weak arguments to obtain benefit:

> Ten cuidado en el interrogatorio. Ese abogado se agarra a un clavo ardiendo.

**Dar en el clavo** means *to guess right, hit the nail on the head*:

> Has dado en el clavo; yo soy el autor de eso.

**Empinar el codo** means *to drink too much*:

> Luis dijo esas tonterías porque había empinado el codo.

**Hablar por los codos** means *to talk too much*:

> ¡Ese chico me vuelve loco! ¡Habla por los codos!

**Cojear del mismo pie** is applied to people who share the same ideas, habits, or weak points:

> No me extraña que estéis de acuerdo, ya que cojeáis del mismo pie.

**Saber de qué pie cojea** expresses that the speaker knows a person's ideas, habits, or weak points:

> No me fío de ti porque sé de qué pie cojeas.

**Ser cosa de** is usually followed by an infinitive. When this is the case, it implies that the action represented by the infinitive is the solution to a certain problem:

> Ya sé que nuestra economía va mal; será cosa de disminuir algunos gastos superfluos.

When followed by a noun or pronoun indicating a person, **ser cosa de** means that the matter referred to in the sentence is the result of somebody's ideas, actions, or intentions :

> ¿Otra vez tenemos que invitar a tu hermana? ¡Seguro que es cosa de tu madre!

**Ser (como) coser y cantar** means that the action referred to in the sentence is very easy:

> Reparar el fregadero fue (como) coser y cantar para mí.

**Venir a cuento** is used to mean that a certain comment is related to what is being said at that moment, has a bearing on it:

> Estamos hablando de economía, así que lo que acabas de decir no viene a cuento.

**Vivir del cuento** indicates that the subject has an easy life without having to work:

> Marta no trabaja; vive del cuento, como todos los miembros de su familia.

**Estar curado de espanto** expresses that the subject has been shocked before and can't therefore be surprised:

> Puedes contarme lo que ha hecho mi hijo esta vez; estoy curada de espanto.

**Dar a entender** means *to make (someone) understand, give to understand*:

> Con esas palabras ella quiso dar a entender que tú le gustabas.

**Dar que decir** implies that a certain action or situation provokes comments or gossip:

> Lo que insinuó el ministro va a dar mucho que decir.

**Darle (a alguien) por ahí** implies that the subject suddenly starts a new activity. It usually refers to decisions made without thinking very much:

Ahora Rosa se dedica a pintar; a ver, le ha dado por ahí.

**Hacerse eco de algo** implies that the subject repeats or uses something heard somewhere:

Ella se hizo eco de los consejos de su profesor.

**Tener eco** usually refers to words that spread easily:

Los poemas de ese autor tuvieron mucho eco en su época.

**Surtir efecto** refers to actions that produce the desired result:

Las nuevas medidas económicas surtirán efecto en un par de años.

**Poner en entredicho** indicates that the subject of this construction is uncertain about the good reputation of somebody/something:

No permito que pongas en entredicho mi conducta profesional.

**Deshacer un entuerto** means *to correct a mistake*, but it is normally used to refer to an injustice:

Tienes que deshacer ese entuerto; ella no se merece que la traten así.

**Dar mala espina** refers to somebody/something considered suspicious or bad:

Ese hombre me da muy mala espina. Creo que nos está siguiendo.

**Pasar factura** refers to actions or activities that will result in some damage in the future:

Tus excesos con el alcohol y el tabaco algún día te pasarán factura.

**Atizar el fuego** refers to comments that cause a quarrel to get worse:

¡No vengas tú ahora a atizar el fuego! ¿No ves que ya no están discutiendo?

**Pegar fuego** means *to set fire (to something)*:

El muy imbécil le pegó fuego a la casa.

**Hacer furor** refers to something that becomes very fashionable:

Sus diseños hicieron furor entre las jovencitas.

**Con ganas** means *extremely*:

> Ese hombre es rico con ganas.

**Tenerle ganas a alguien** means that the subject has a great desire to take revenge on somebody:

> ¡Le tengo unas ganas a Pablo! ¡El otro día me pintorreó el diccionario!

**Dar gato por liebre** is used when somebody sells something of low quality for the same price as top-quality merchandise. It can be used figuratively:

> ¡Esta carne por cincuenta dólares! ¡Ese carnicero te ha dado gato por liebre!

**Llevarse el gato al agua** generally means *to win* and it can be used in a wide range of contexts:

> Cuando ella y yo discutimos, ella siempre se lleva el gato al agua.

**Ir al grano** means *to get to the point*:

> ¿Por qué no vas al grano y te dejas de rodeos?

**Echar el guante a alguien** means *to catch* and it refers to criminals, but figuratively it can refer to anybody who deserves a lesson:

> Cuando le eche el guante a mi hijo, ¡se va a enterar de quién soy yo!

**Sentar como un guante** refers to items of clothing that fit perfectly:

> Esa chaqueta te sienta como un guante.

**De lo que no hay** means *unique*; it usually refers to bad or negative qualities:

> Mi sobrino es de lo que no hay; ha suspendido todas las asignaturas por tercera vez.

**Donde los/las haya** is placed after adjectives to reinforce or emphasize their meaning:

> Mi hijo es travieso donde los haya.

**Hacer aguas** is used to refer to something that is getting worse and worse:

> El matrimonio de Pedro y Yasmina está haciendo aguas.

**Hacer la vista gorda** means *to pretend ignorance, look the other way*:

> El policía hizo la vista gorda y pudimos aparcar delante de la tienda.

**Ser hora de** corresponds to the English construction *to be about time*. With this meaning, **ser hora de** can be preceded by the word **ya** and is always followed by present subjunctive forms if the verb **ser** is in the present. **Ir siendo hora de** is often used instead of **ser hora de**, especially when the activity proposed is urgent:

> Ya va siendo hora de que limpies tu habitación.
> Ya es hora de que nos cuentes la verdad.

**Ser hora de** or **ir siendo hora de** can also be followed by infinitives to mean *to be time to*:

> Ya es hora de marcharnos.
> Ya va siendo hora de empezar el trabajo.

**Hacerse a la idea** means *to accept a situation, get used to the idea*:

> Me costó aceptar que mi hija quería ser policía, pero ya me he hecho a la idea.

**Dar igual** means *to be all the same to*, expressing a lack of preference or concern:

> Puedes hacer café o té, me da igual.
> Yo sé que ella se está viendo con ese chico, pero me da igual.

**Valer un imperio** is used to refer to somebody with extraordinary merits or something that is very valuable:

> Esa mujer vale un imperio; trabaja, estudia de noche y cuida a sus hermanos.

**¡Dónde va a parar!** can refer to people, things, situations, and so on. It expresses that there is no possible comparison between one and the other:

> Este coche es mucho más rápido que el otro, dónde va a parar.

**Ir a parar** means *to come to a stop or end*:

> La pelota fue a parar al tejado de los vecinos.
> Este conducto va a parar a unos estanques que hay fuera.

Figuratively, **ir a parar** means *to get at*, especially in conversation:

> ¿Dónde quieres ir a parar con esos comentarios?

**Ir para largo** expresses that a situation is going to take a long time. It is usually connected with the idea of waiting for something to happen:

El médico suele tardar veinte minutos por paciente y yo tengo el número quince, así que esto va para largo.

**Vete tú a saber** expresses uncertainty or ignorance about something. It can also denote a lack of interest:

Ya sé que dicen que Pepe se lo encontró por casualidad, pero vete tú a saber.

**Traer en jaque a alguien** means *to cause great difficulties to someone*:

El nuevo bloqueo trae en jaque al gobierno de ese país.

Figuratively, **traer en jaque a alguien** refers to giving someone a large number of activities that have to be done without giving him or her time to relax:

Mis hijos me traen en jaque todo el día.

**Jugarla** means *to deceive* or *to trick*:

Lo que llevas en esa bolsa no es lo que compraste; te la han jugado.

**Romper una lanza por** usually means *to defend*:

Quiero romper una lanza por Juan; creo que estáis siendo injustos con él.

**Dar largas** implies that the subject delays something on purpose:

Veo que le estás dando largas a mi solicitud.

**Hablar largo y tendido** implies having a long conversation with many important details:

Hablaron largo y tendido sobre la juventud de hoy día.

**Dar la lata** expresses that the subject insists too much or talks too much about something in an annoying way:

Mi mujer me estuvo dando la lata con la dichosa fiesta.

**Irse de la lengua** implies saying something that shouldn't be said. It is connected with the idea of revealing a secret:

La policía nos atrapó porque él se fue de la lengua.

**Morderse la lengua** is used when somebody doesn't say something in order to avoid an unpleasant situation:

Cuando ella me preguntó lo que opinaba de su vestido, tuve que morderme la lengua.

**Tirar de la lengua** refers to the use of a stratagem to make somebody speak or give an opinion:

No me tires de la lengua, porque como diga lo que pienso, nos vamos a pelear.

**Limar asperezas** implies eliminating small problems before an important matter is discussed:

Representantes del gobierno y los sindicatos han limado asperezas antes de las reuniones de la semana que viene.

**Hacerse un lío** means *to get all mixed up*:

Me estoy haciendo un lío con tantos nombres.

**Como quien oye llover** is used when somebody hears something without paying attention:

Se lo dije al director, pero me miró como quien oye llover.

**Llover sobre mojado** refers to adding one problem to another problem:

Aquí llueve sobre mojado; ahora el gobierno va a subir los impuestos de los carburantes.

**Dar a luz** means *to give birth*:

Ella dio a luz a un niño precioso.

**Salir a la luz** means *to become public*:

Al final salió a la luz que eran amantes.

EJERCICIO

## 12·1

*Fill in the blanks with suitable idioms. Pay attention to the clue in parentheses.*

EXAMPLE     Todo salió _____ (boca).

Todo salió ___*a pedir de boca*___ .

1. Esa mujer me hizo _____ (cabeza). ¡Me enamoré perdidamente!

2. No debiste insultar al profesor. Eso te va a _____ (caro).

3. Juan las _____ (canutas). Tuvo que vivir con 200 dólares al mes.

4. Esto _____ (camino) de convertirse en un problema sin solución posible.

5. El marido de Ana es _____ (bote). Piensa que Shakespeare fue un famoso pirata.

6. ¡Aquí el que _____ (bacalao) soy yo! ¡Yo soy el que manda!

7. Ya sabemos que eres el mejor de todos nosotros. No _____ (abuela).

8. Localizar a tu hermana en alguna discoteca es como _____ (aguja).

**EJERCICIO 12·2**

*Following each sentence write the idiomatic expression that you could use instead of the phrase in quotation marks.*

1. Antonio "tuvo muchísimos problemas" con su hijo por culpa de las drogas.

   _____

2. Luis "se volvió loco" cuando su mujer le dejó.

   _____

3. Pedro "gana su dinero" cargando y descargando camiones.

   _____

4. Mis padres "han gastado demasiado dinero" esta Navidad.

   _____

5. "Me divertí muchísimo."

   _____

6. Mi novia "alternativamente me mima y me trata fatal".

   _____

7. Este mes tengo muchos clientes. "Estoy ganando mucho dinero."

   _____

8. "¡Ya entiendo!" ¡Has sido tú quien ha comprado los pasteles!

   _____

*Find and correct any mistakes.*

1. Mis conocimientos del francés son de andar en casa.

2. Vamos a tomar unas cervezas para abrir nuestras bocas.

3. Tu opinión demuestra que has oído campanas y no sabes dónde.

4. El restaurante estaba bote en bote.

5. Mi suegra me da una de arena y otra de cal.

6. Por lo visto di en blanco, porque ella se puso muy nerviosa.

7. Perdona, me he quedado en blanco. ¿Qué quieres decir?

8. Me di baja, porque tenía un enorme resfriado.

*Fill in the blanks with suitable idioms using the information in parentheses.*

1. Elena se _____ (lío) cuando le pregunté cuál era la capital de Rusia.

2. Espero que no te _____ (lengua) cuando venga Ana.

3. Les he pedido que me presten el suyo, pero aún no me han respondido. Es obvio que me están _____ (largas).

4. Le he comprado la bici a mi hijo para que me deje de _____ (lata).

5. Ella es mucho más guapa que su hermana, dónde _____ (parar).

6. El negocio está _____ (aguas). Cada vez tenemos menos clientes.

7. Ese restaurante es caro _____ (haya).

8. Dejémonos de circunloquios y _____ (grano).

EJERCICIO

**12·5**

*Following each sentence write the idiomatic expression that you could use
instead of the phrase in quotation marks.*

1. Veo que me estás escuchando "sin prestarme atención".

   _____

2. El profesor se enteró de que lo hice yo, porque "Pablo me delató".

   _____

3. Carlos siempre "me está molestando" con sus opiniones futbolísticas.

   _____

4. Tendremos que tener paciencia. El médico dice que "esto va a durar bastante".

   _____

5. La mujer "trajo gemelos".

   _____

6. Le han dado el puesto a Jorge. Está claro que "te han engañado".

   _____

7. Mi mujer "es estupenda". Yo soy muy feliz con ella.

   _____

8. Los terroristas "atosigan a la policía".

   _____

*Find and correct any mistakes.*

1. Tu respuesta es correcta. Has tirado el clavo.

2. Espero que consigamos limpiar asperezas.

3. Tuve que romperme la lengua para que ella no se sintiera mal.

4. Deberías hacerte a la idea de que lo nuestro no puede ser.

5. Les vi robando caramelos, pero hice la vista gorda.

6. ¡Estás borracho! ¡Has estado subiendo el codo otra vez!

7. Los conductos del agua van a parar a un río cercano.

8. Sí sabía la respuesta; lo que pasa es que me di un lío.

# Answer key

## 1 Object pronouns and omission of subject pronouns

**1-1** 1. Le, la   2. les (**Los/Las** *can never be used as indirect object pronouns.*)   3. le/lo (*Originally,* **le** *and* **les** *were correct only as indirect object pronouns, but now the Real Academia de la Lengua Española accepts their use as direct object pronouns, as long as they don't refer to animals or things.*)   4. le   5. Le   6. lo   7. la   8. les, Les/Los

**1-2** 1. le, lo   2. -, la   3. te, te   4. -   5. me, Lo   6. -, Le, le   7. me, le, lo   8. se

**1-3** 1. Buenos días, soy Marco. Hola, yo soy Felipe.   2. Soy enfermera. Yo soy secretaria.   3. Yo no lo he hecho.   4. ¿Es usted de Los Ángeles? (*It is possible to omit the subject pronoun, but it is advisable not to do so with third-person forms.*) No, soy de Nueva York.

**1-4** 1. Yo voy a ir a los lagos. Yo tengo que quedarme en casa.   2. *No subject pronouns are necessary.*   3. *No subject pronouns are necessary, but in the first sentence it is better to say* ¿Puede usted... ?

**1-5** 1. le/lo van   2. Correct   3. les quise (*However, in colloquial Spanish, it is very common to use a singular object pronoun when it is followed by* a + *plural indication:* No le quiero decir nada a mis padres.)   4. no me lo dijo   5. le hagas   6. Correct   7. *The second* **él** *is not necessary.*   8. les gusta

**1-6** 1. Paco no nos la va a querer instalar. (O: Paco no va a querer instalárnosla.)   2. Yo tuve que dárselo. (O: Yo se lo tuve que dar.)   3. No me la han traído todavía.   4. Pepe se lo regaló.   5. Se los vendí.   6. Si yo fuera tú, yo no se lo diría.   7. Juan no se los tiene que devolver. (O: Juan no tiene que devolvérselos.)   8. Ana me los va a traer esta mañana. (O: Ana va a traérmelos esta mañana.)

**1-7** 1. *There is no other possibility, because verbs such as* **gustar** *take indirect objects and* **lo** *is a direct object.*   2. *There is no other possibility, because this sentence doesn't refer to a human being.*   3. **los invitaré** *is another possibility.*   4. *There is no other possibility since* **aterrar** *is like the verb* **gustar**.   5. **lo han castigado** *is another possibility.*   6. *There is no other possibility since* **la** *can't be used as an indirect object.*

**1-8** 1. A Luis no le salieron muy bien las cosas. (O: A Luis no le salieron las cosas muy bien. o: Las cosas no le salieron muy bien a Luis.)   2. Yo no fui quien se lo contó a Antonio.   3. A mi novia le encantan las películas de miedo.   4. Ana no nos lo ha prestado.   5. ¿Quién se lo encargó al mecánico?   6. Paco dice que no le gustan mucho.

**1-9** 1. She gave it to us.   2. Paco sent it to his brother.   3. I told her (about it).   4. The teacher wants to see you at seven.   5. It's me, Juan. Let me in.   6. Mrs. Antúnez made coffee for us. (Or: Mrs. Antúnez made us coffee.)   7. Carla was waiting for us in the living room.   8. Juan was telling us a joke when she called him.    9. María was explaining it to them.    10. They didn't want to show it to you.

1-10    1. Tendrán que hablar con nosotros primero.    2. Ella no quería venir conmigo.    3. ¿Por qué no quiere Patricia trabajar contigo?    4. Tú puedes dársela.    5. Él lo hizo para nosotros.    6. Le/Lo he visto en la oficina.    7. Le he dicho que no podemos ir con él.    8. A ella le encanta el fútbol.    9. Le/Lo llevaré a su habitación.    10. ¡No soporto a Pedro!    11. Les pregunté si ya habían visto mi casa y respondieron que ya la habían visto.    12. Las necesito ahora. No puedo leer nada sin ellas.

# 2    *Some/any* and other determiners

2-1    1. unas/algunas    2. un montón de    3. ha venido (*When* **nadie** *is placed before the verb sequence,* **no** *is not used before the verb.*)    4. cualquier    5. poca    6. los dos    7. todos los días/cada día    8. todos

2-2    1. alguien    2. unas cuantas/unas pocas    3. todos los    4. cada    5. poca    6. Cualquiera    7. montones de    8. ninguno de los dos

2-3    1. Todos los    2. nadie    3. todo    4. cada    5. un poco de    6. montón de    7. ninguna    8. alguien

2-4    1. de mis amigos    2. tendrá que (*The subject* **Uno de los dos** *is singular.*)    3. no queda ningún asiento libre. (**Ningún** *has to be singular; there is no plural form.*)    4. Correct    5. todas las    6. Correct    7. Nadie ha venido    8. Correct

2-5    1. Hemos registrado cada rincón.    2. No he tomado nada de alcohol.    3. ¿Vio Ana a alguien entre los matorrales? (O: ¿Vio alguien a Ana entre los matorrales?)    4. Algunos de mis compañeros han sido despedidos.    5. Algún día serás el dueño de todo esto.    6. No ha llamado nadie desde ayer.

2-6    1. Casi no hay cerveza en el sótano.    2. Algunos de mis amigos participaron en la manifestación.    3. Suelo entrenar cada día.    4. Uno de los dos chicos tendrá que limpiar el patio.    5. No ha solicitado nadie ese empleo todavía.    6. No tienes nada que temer.

2-7    1. La, de    2. Unos    3. en    4. lo    5. un, de    6. de los    7. a    8. de

2-8    1. G    2. E    3. F    4. H    5. D    6. C    7. A    8. B

2-9    1. I don't want to do anything this afternoon.    2. There were a lot of people in the store. 3. There are very few bears left in this forest.    4. I usually see them every day.    5. The postman comes at ten every day.    6. Every time I see them I get nervous.    7. They have drunk all the wine.    8. Nobody has been here this week.    9. We haven't been able to do anything.    10. There is something strange on that table.    11. I would like to go somewhere interesting.    12. They weren't anywhere.

2-10    1. No podemos ver nada desde aquí.    2. No quedan muchos clientes.    3. Él tiene muchos juegos en su ordenador.    4. Hubo algunos problemas cuando empezó la huelga. (*Inversion is very common in this type of sentence, although it is possible to say* ... cuando la huelga empezó.) 5. Veo que no tienes cerveza en tu vaso.    6. Algo extraño está ocurriendo/sucediendo/pasando. 7. Algunas personas creen/piensan que hay extraterrestres en el gobierno.    8. No voy a invertir más dinero en esa empresa.    9. Algún día seré el jefe.    10. De alguna forma/manera consiguieron ver al presidente.    11. Debe de haber alguien ahí/allí dentro.    12. Comamos en algún lugar/sitio tranquilo.

# 3 Adjectives

**3-1**    1. el marrón    2. los ciegos    3. marroquíes (*Words ending in a strong* **-í** *or* **-ú** *take* **-es** *in the plural.*)    4. cada vez más difícil    5. Cuanto, -    6. más fuerte    7. - (*If you invert the order of the adjective and noun, then the preposition* **de** *is necessary:* Es un problema difícil de solucionar.)    8. el amarillo

**3-2**    1. israelí, israelíes    2. andaluza, andaluces/andaluzas    3. verde, verdes    4. amarilla, amarillos/amarillas    5. japonesa, japoneses/japonesas    6. española, españoles/españolas    7. exigente, exigentes    8. ágil, ágiles

*Remember that adjectives of nationality or region ending in a consonant do have a feminine form.*

**3-3**    1. Correct    2. Correct    3. quedan menos bosques    4. que jamás he visto    5. Correct    6. comida francesa    7. lo guapa    8. por tu parte

**3-4**    1. cuidadoso/cuidadosa    2. próxima    3. Lejano    4. listo    5. cara    6. fabulosa    7. Medio    8. última

**3-5**    1. Antonio no es tan inteligente como su hermana. (O: La hermana de Antonio es [mucho] más inteligente que él.)    2. Juan tiene muchos más suspensos que yo. (O: Yo no tengo tantos suspensos como Juan.)    3. Ésta es la cantidad más alta (o: la máxima cantidad) que estoy dispuesto a ofrecer. (O: No estoy dispuesto a ofrecer una cantidad más alta que ésta.)    4. Lo único/máximo que te pido es que me ayudes con esto.    5. Carlos es el que menos cualidades tiene de todos los candidatos. (O: Carlos tiene menos cualidades que los demás candidatos. Los demás candidatos tienen más cualidades que Carlos.)    6. Fue la experiencia más aterradora que tuve jamás.    7. Jorge es mucho más fuerte que sus compañeros de clase.    8. El paciente está hoy mejor que ayer. (O: El paciente estaba ayer peor que hoy.)

**3-6**    1. Cuanto más alto te hagas, mejor jugarás al baloncesto.    2. Cada vez hay menos casas baratas en esta zona.    3. No lo entiendo. Cuanto más invierto, más pierdo.    4. Cada día estás más guapa.    5. Cuanto más me esfuerzo, peores son mis resultados.    6. Cuanto más lo leo, menos lo entiendo.    7. Los precios están cada vez más altos.    8. Cuanto más tienen, más quieren.

**3-7**    1. La película tiene demasiadas escenas inconvenientes (como) para que los niños la vean.    2. El coche es demasiado viejo para hacer (o: para poder hacer) un viaje largo con él.    3. Ese restaurante es demasiado caro para que les invitemos ahí.    4. Este documento es demasiado técnico para que Carla lo entienda sin un abogado. (O: ... para que Carla lo pueda entender sin un abogado.)    5. Este curso es demasiado fácil para que Tony aprenda lo suficiente.    6. Ana es demasiado ambiciosa para contentarse con tan poca cosa.    7. Carlos está demasiado ocupado para atendernos (o: para poder atendernos) mañana. (O: Carlos está demasiado ocupado para que nos atienda mañana. Carlos está demasiado ocupado para que nos pueda atender mañana.)    8. Ese médico es demasiado viejo para operar a nuestro hijo. (*The use of* **como** *is not compulsory.*)

**3-8**    1. rarísimo, rarito    2. ligerísimo, ligerito    3. fortísimo, fuertecito    4. lentísimo, lentito    5. exageradísimo, exageradito    6. carísimo, carito    7. baratísimo, baratito    8. peligrosísimo, peligrosito

**3-9** 1. The film I saw last night is very, very good (the very best).    2. My grandmother is much better than last week.    3. That is too dangerous for the child to do.    4. It's the worst stage play I have ever seen.    5. My car isn't as fast as yours. Yours is very, very fast.    6. The rent we pay for this apartment is very, very high.    7. I have never been in the Near East.    8. This bus is a bit/rather slow.    9. It's good to get up early.    10. It's bad to smoke so much.    11. It is very important that they know this.    12. She needn't clean the rooms. (Or: It is not necessary that she clean the rooms. It is not necessary for her to clean the rooms.)

**3-10** 1. Es muy urgente que él venga de inmediato.    2. Esto es demasiado difícil para que él lo intente.    3. Es el peor libro que he leído en mi vida.    4. Vuestra casa es mucho más grande que la nuestra.    5. No es muy inteligente hacer eso.    6. El examen fue dificilísimo. (*You can also use adverbs to qualify the word* **examen**: El examen fue extremadamente/sumamente difícil.)    7. El artículo que leí en el periódico esta mañana es buenísimo.    8. Son paupérrimos.    9. Ese restaurante es baratito/algo barato.    10. Ella es mucho más alta que su hermana.    11. Él no está tan cualificado como su hermano.    12. Les vi en la otra orilla.

# 4 Adverbs

**4-1** 1. tarde   2. recién   3. realmente   4. bastante   5. diariamente/a diario   6. a la izquierda   7. casi nunca   8. últimamente/recientemente   9. demasiado   10. mucho

**4-2** 1. alto   2. pronto   3. Fundamentalmente   4. Correct   5. repartes correctamente/justamente   6. baratos   7. entrar gratis   8. Os espero de vuelta   9. Correct   10. Correct

**4-3** 1. pronto   2. probable   3. completamente   4. sumamente   5. fuerte   6. bajito   7. demasiado   8. amigable   9. regularmente   10. Apenas

**4-4** 1. gratis   2. recién   3. injustamente   4. mal   5. fríamente   6. temprano   7. tarde   8. cerca   9. regularmente   10. Apenas

**4-5** 1. No tenemos suficiente tiempo para (poder) terminar los informes. (*It is not advisable to use* **bastante** *in negative sentences when a noun follows.*)    2. No gano suficiente dinero para (poder) ir a restaurantes. (*If* **dinero** *is omitted, it is then possible to say*: No gano lo bastante/lo suficiente [como] para poder ir a restaurantes.)    3. El tiempo no está (lo) suficientemente/lo bastante bueno (como) para ir a la playa.    4. Las maletas no son (lo) suficientemente ligeras (como) para que María las pueda llevar. (O: ... [como] para que María las lleve. **Lo** *can be used with* **bastante** *in negative sentences when no noun follows*: Las maletas no son lo bastante ligeras... )    5. No estudiaste lo suficiente para aprobar.    6. No nos han enviado suficiente material para todos.    7. Antonio no es (lo) suficientemente/lo bastante tranquilo (como) para lidiar con niños. (*In this type of sentence,* **suficientemente** *can be preceded by* **lo**; *bastante can't be used without it.*)    8. Elena no tiene suficiente preparación (como) para conseguir ese empleo.

**4-6** 1. Mi madre acababa de terminar la comida.    2. Acabo de coger los discos que tenías preparados.    3. Lo acabamos de decidir.    4. Juan acababa de hablar con Antonio cuando se encontró conmigo.    5. Acabo de estar allí.    6. Les acabo de llamar.    7. Felipe me acababa de decir que no me quedara con los libros.    8. Tomás acaba de marcharse.

**4-7** 1. sólo   2. sólo   3. solo   4. Sólo, solo   5. sólo, solas   6. sólo   7. sólo   8. sola

**4-8** 1. suavemente   2. mensualmente   3. fríamente   4. fácilmente *is better*   5. regular (*the only possibility in this case*)   6. claramente   7. regularmente, semanalmente   8. profundamente   9. cuidadosamente   10. pronto (*the only possibility in this case*)

**4-9**  1. He isn't strong enough to do that.   2. Juan behaved very coolly.   3. If they come soon/early, we will go and play tennis.   4. All this is free. Ana gave it to me.   5. I have just seen a terrible accident.   6. My secretary is extremely accurate.   7. You are right. The restaurant is on the right.   8. Turn left at the traffic light.   9. I only/just need two hours to do it.   10. Pedro is highly qualified.

**4-10**  1. Es probable que lleguen más tarde.   2. Los prisioneros se escaparon (sin problemas, fácilmente, etc.).   3. Ella está equivocada. Pedro no acaba de estar aquí.   4. Creo que él lo hizo a sangre fría.   5. El jefe me trató muy amigablemente. (O: El jefe me trató de forma muy amigable.)   6. Te prestaré mi ordenador siempre que prometas que no vas a jugar con él.   7. ¿Te llevará mucho?   8. Ella no nos ha visitado últimamente/recientemente.   9. Creo que eso es suficientemente justo.   10. Estaremos aquí a las doce en punto.   11. Casi no quedaba nada. (O: Apenas quedaba nada.)   12. Yo llevaba ropa de abrigo (o: ropa de invierno), porque hacía mucho frío.   13. Estaba exhausto/agotado/cansadísimo después del partido.   14. El agujero no es (lo) suficientemente/lo bastante profundo.   15. Estudia esto atentamente (o: con mucha atención). Es importantísimo.

# 5   Commands and requests

**5-1**  1. Los clientes tienen que abandonar los grandes almacenes a las seis en punto.   2. No se permite la entrada a menores de dieciocho años en esta discoteca.   3. Chicos, no juguéis entre las flores.   4. Limpiemos esto antes de que Pepe se entere.   5. No deje usted el equipaje en el vestíbulo.   6. Los formularios han de ser entregados en recepción.   7. No te permito que bebas alcohol en tu cumpleaños. (O: No te permito beber... )   8. Que ellas no laven al bebé.

**5-2**  1. permites/dejas   2. de dejarme   3. pudiera   4. gustaría   5. Podrías   6. apetece/apetecería (*The conditional can sound more polite.*)   7. Se me permite abrir/Se permite que abra   8. Querrías

**5-3**  1. venir   2. se permite   3. deben/tienen que/han de dejar   4. Callaos   5. Que vengas   6. Correct   7. fuera   8. Correct

**5-4**  1. Could you show me the photos, please?   2. Let me use yours, please.   3. The clients will have to pay in cash.   4. Drinking alcohol is not allowed.   5. Good morning. I would like to talk with the manager, please.   6. Let's put it behind the door.   7. Let Luisa do the rest.   8. Let's not talk about that in front of him/in his presence. (**Delante de él** *literally means in front of him.*)   9. Would you be so kind as to hold the door, please?   10. Do you sell books in Spanish?

**5-5**  1. ¿Me puede pasar el agua mineral, por favor?   2. No vendamos la casa todavía.   3. Que Felipe compre las bebidas. (*Inversion is common*: Que compre las bebidas Felipe o: Que compre Felipe las bebidas.)   4. Los estudiantes rellenarán los formularios a lápiz.   5. Me preguntaba si te ibas a comer esas patatas. (O: Me estaba preguntando si te ibas a comer esas patatas.)   6. Me gustaría que me explicara esto.   7. Necesito que me lleves.   8. ¿Me quieres alargar los clavos, por favor?   9. Chicos, no habléis tan fuerte.   10. Permítame que le abra la puerta, señora.

# 6   Modal constructions

**6-1**  1. Es mejor que no contrates a ese abogado.   2. Sería mejor que no hablaras con Mari sobre este tema.   3. No deberías hacer que vieran que eres el mejor.   4. No debes quedarte con la amarilla.    5. Yo que tú, no alquilaría un apartamento en esta playa.    6. Es mucho mejor que no te fumes un cigarrillo.    7. Sería mejor que no intentaras escalar esa montaña.    8. Te aconsejo que no te cases con ella.

6-2    1. Debía de    2. hacía    3. tenías    4. podía ser    5. lleguen    6. Deberías    7. estuviera    8. Tenía que

6-3    1. arregles    2. que intenten    3. Correct    4. Correct    5. Correct    6. Correct    7. Correct    8. ¿Qué tal si nos

6-4    1. I suggest you put on the other tie. (Or: I suggest your putting on the other tie.)    2. What about renting a boat?    3. They must have been very tired. That's why they went to bed so early.    4. You shouldn't have prepared so much food. (*This sentence can also be translated as* You needn't have prepared so much food, *as* **no debiste** *can be either a reproach or a reference to an unnecessary action.*)    5. If I were you, I would choose the yellow one.    6. Let's talk with Juan before making (any) strange decisions.    7. You should have gotten off at the other station.    8. You should have had breakfast; you wouldn't be so hungry now.    9. You needn't have come, but thanks.    10. I think you should have it looked at.

6-5    1. Usted no tenía que haber ayudado a Andrea. (No tenía haber ayudado *can sound like a reproach; therefore it is better to use* No hacía falta que usted ayudara, *which simply refers to a past action that wasn't necessary.*)    2. Sugiero que pruebes el coche/auto primero.    3. Si yo fuera vosotros, no me quedaría/alojaría en ese hotel.    4. Usted no debería leer esta clase de libro/este tipo de libro. (O: No debería usted leer... o: Sería mejor que no leyera usted... )    5. Deberías ahorrar más dinero si quieres comprar una casa.    6. Debes de/Tienes que haber oído la noticia. (*If the reference is to a more remote past,* Debiste de/Tuviste que oír la noticia *is better.*)    7. ¿Qué tal si les hacemos una visita?    8. Pongamos la mesa, ¿vale/de acuerdo? (O: Vamos a poner la mesa... )    9. Yo sugeriría pedir cordero.    10. Le aconsejo que beba menos.    11. ¿Por qué no llevas (o: te pones) el vestido que te compré la semana pasada?    12. ¿Les decimos que vengan con nosotros?

# 7    Impersonal sentences and the passive

7-1    1. Las paredes están siendo pintadas por Antonio.    2. El trabajo no pudo ser terminado (por ellos).    3. Las agresiones de los manifestantes tuvieron que ser repelidas por la policía.    4. Esa ley ha sido derogada por el nuevo gobierno.    5. Todos los nuevos modelos tendrán que ser revisados por los fabricantes.    6. La leche nos es traída a la puerta todos los días por el lechero.    7. El teléfono acaba de ser instalado.    8. ¿Qué fue comprado por los vecinos?    9. Todos esos alumnos van a ser expulsados por el director.    10. La combinación no habría sido averiguada por ella.

7-2    1. Es probable que esta carretera sea cortada. (O: Es probable que corten esta carretera.)    2. Me cortan el pelo una vez cada dos meses.    3. Nos están cortando el césped.    4. Ayer no me trajeron el periódico.    5. Me han robado la bicicleta.    6. Esta casa necesita ser limpiada en profundidad.    7. Presiento que nos están siguiendo.    8. No les invitaron.    9. Elena no quiso que la llevaran al hospital.    10. Ayer cambié las ruedas delanteras. (O: Ayer, las ruedas delanteras me fueron cambiadas.)

7-3    1. Están tratando a Carlos en el hospital.    2. Asaltaron a la pobre mujer dos veces en el mismo día. (*It is possible to put* **a la pobre mujer** *in different places in the sentence:* A la pobre mujer la asaltaron dos veces en el mismo día o: Asaltaron dos veces en el mismo día a la pobre mujer.)

3. La policía ha clausurado las instalaciones.    4. No van a poder liberar a Javier este sábado.
5. Los deberían haber corregido en rojo.    6. No tenían que haber admitido a nadie ese día.
7. Eso lo fabricaron muy mal.    8. Nos la están explicando en este momento.    9. Deberían haber
puesto a alguien a controlar la entrada.    10. Me van a nombrar jefe de departamento.

**7-4**    1. expulsados    2. Correct    3. pintando    4. Se dice que Juan tiene la solución.    5. está muy mal
pintada    6. Correct    7. Me han dicho    8. Se supone    9. se han traducido    10. Correct

**7-5**    1. se descubrieron/fueron descubiertas    2. han sido incrementadas    3. ha    4. siendo    5. se
fabrican/son fabricados    6. hablan/se habla    7. necesitan    8. fue descubierta    9. entrarán
10. va a

**7-6**    1. We are having our carpets cleaned. (Or: Our carpets are being cleaned.)    2. I had the
purchase(s) brought home yesterday.    3. Such cars are no longer made.    4. The patient is being
operated on at this moment. (Or: The patient is having an operation at this moment.)    5. They
should already have been repaired.    6. All the lights were turned on.    7. All the lights were
on.    8. The crime hasn't been investigated yet.

**7-7**    1. Van a construir dos nuevas casas en esa zona. (O: Dos nuevas casas van a ser construidas en esa
zona.)    2. ¿Cuándo te revisaron el coche? (O: ¿Cuándo revisaste el coche?)    3. Se dice que ella
trabaja para esa compañía. (O: Dicen que ella... )    4. Se supone que él es el jefe.    5. Los niños
deberían haber sido vigilados. (O: Deberían haber vigilado a los niños.)    6. Las luces están
todavía apagadas (o: todavía están apagadas), pero las van a encender muy pronto. (O: ... pero van
a ser encendidas muy pronto.)    7. Se hace/Le hacen los vestidos en Nueva York.    8. Se lo debería
haber investigado un especialista. (*This type of subject-verb inversion is common, but it is possible
to say:* Un especialista se lo debería haber investigado.)    9. No se le permitirá a nadie entrar sin
entrada. (O: A nadie se le permitirá entrar sin entrada.)    10. Mari no puede haber sido vista allí.
(O: No pueden haber visto a Mari allí.)

# 8 Relative pronouns and conjunctions

**8-1**    1. que/cuales (*In less formal Spanish,* **cual/cuales** *is less common.*)    2. cuya    3. que/quien/el
cual    4. lo que/qué    5. lo cual    6. lo que/lo cual    7. quien

**8-2**    1. Carla es la doctora que me atendió el otro día.    2. Antonio, que/quien/el cual adora los
animales, quiere ser veterinario.    3. El señor Sánchez, para el que/el cual yo trabajé el año
pasado, vendrá mañana.    4. Mi profesor de español, que/quien/el cual es muy simpático, me ha
regalado este libro.    5. Ése es el coche con el que/el cual gané la carrera.    6. El bar desde el que/
el cual te llamé era muy ruidoso. (O: El bar desde donde te llamé... )    7. En diciembre
organizamos una gran fiesta en la que/cual hubo hasta payasos.

**8-3**    1. A pesar de que/Aunque los resultados de este año han sido muy malos, esperamos mejorar el
año que viene. (O: Los resultados de este año han sido muy malos; no obstante, esperamos... )
2. A pesar de que/Aunque no necesito ayuda de nadie, puedes echarme una mano. (O: No
necesito ayuda de nadie; no obstante, puedes... )    3. A pesar de que/Aunque Marta no tenía nada
de dinero, compró un anillo de diamantes. (O: A pesar de no tener nada de dinero, Marta
compró... o: Marta no tenía nada de dinero; no obstante, compró... )    4. Entraré en esa discoteca,
aunque el portero se pelee conmigo.    5. Ella no pudo conseguir ese empleo porque (o: debido a
que) tenía más de cincuenta años.    6. Paco no pudo jugar el partido porque tenía una grave
lesión.    7. Justo cuando yo estaba dando un paseo por el parque, cayó el helicóptero.

**8-4**    1. Correct    2. A pesar de que/Aunque ella es muy mayor...    3. Juan no invitó a Tomás a pesar de ser muy amigos. (O: Juan no invitó a Tomás, aunque eran muy amigos.)    4. Correct
5. Correct    6. No necesito ese préstamo; por tanto, no pienso pedirlo. (O: ... ; así que no pienso pedirlo.)    7. Como no me gusta...

**8-5**    1. A pesar de que/Aunque    2. a pesar de que    3. Si/Como/Ya que    4. a pesar de    5. aunque
6. aunque    7. A medida    8. ni, ni    9. por tanto/así que    10. A pesar de

*Aunque is usually preceded by a comma when no subjunctive follows.*

**8-6**    1. In spite of the rain, we succeeded in finishing the tennis match.    2. I haven't opened the presents yet. (Or: I still haven't opened the presents.)    3. Juan didn't know what had happened so he didn't phone the police.    4. In spite of its being very late, the children didn't go home.
5. Neither Juan nor Luis had been with her.    6. Both Alicia and Pedro visited Roberto in the hospital.    7. Besides having a yacht, Paco has a plane.    8. She is not a nurse but a doctor.    9. The weather was awful yet we decided to go to the mountains. (Or: ... awful; however, we ... )
10. The girl with whom you saw me in the restaurant is one of Pablo's sisters. (Or: The girl you saw me with ... )

**8-7**    1. Paco no fue al restaurante, ya que pensaba que no llevaba la ropa adecuada/correcta.    2. Tanto Felipe como Andrea tuvieron que repetir el examen.    3. Además de trabajar en este hospital, Juan trabaja en una clínica privada.    4. O Madrid o París organizarán los próximos Juegos Olímpicos.    5. Tenemos este coche/auto desde que (nos) vinimos a vivir aquí.    6. Paco no puede haber visto nada, ya que no estaba allí en ese momento. (*If the sentence refers to a more remote past,* **no debió de/pudo ver nada** *is better.*)    7. No tengo mucho tiempo; sin embargo, te ayudaré.    8. Tomás, que/quien es arquitecto, diseñará nuestra casa. (**Que** *is more common but* **quien** *is possible.*)    9. El señor González, para el que/para quien/para el cual trabajo, viene a cenar esta noche. (*Spanish speakers don't often use* **el cual**, *unless they want the sentence to sound formal.*)    10. La mujer cuyo marido solicitó el empleo quiere verte.

# 9    Reported speech

**9-1**    1. Juan le dijo a Antonio que no le iba muy bien con los estudios.    2. Ella me dijo que creía que iba a haber una manifestación en esa calle al día siguiente.    3. Yo le dije a mi novia que no nos podíamos ver allí esa/aquella noche.    4. Mi profesor me dijo que esos ejercicios tenían que estar hechos para el día siguiente.    5. Él dijo que aún no sabía si podría pagar todas esas/aquellas facturas antes del lunes siguiente.    6. El juez le dijo que le condenaba a tres meses de prisión menor.    7. Ella dijo que no había estado haciendo nada importante esa/aquella tarde.    8. Yo les dije que yo no estuve/había estado en el colegio el día anterior, porque estaba enfermo. (*Remember that the imperfect doesn't change in the reported sentence.*)

**9-2**    1. Juan le preguntó a Paco que con quién iba a pasar esa Navidad.    2. Marta me preguntó si ya había regresado mi hermana.    3. Les pregunté que por qué no se pasaban y se tomaban una copa.    4. Ella me preguntó (que) en qué universidad estudió/había estudiado mi hermano. (*The use of* **que** *in reported questions is common, especially when pronouns and prepositions follow.*)    5. El policía me preguntó si había bebido mucho esa/aquella noche.    6. Mi madre me preguntó que a qué se debía que estuviera allí tan temprano.    7. Yo les pregunté si les apetecía cenar con nosotros.    8. El profesor preguntó que quién descubrió América.

**9-3**    1. Ella me dijo que sujetara eso hasta que se bajara de la escalera.    2. Yo les dije que hablaran más bajito para que no se despertara el bebé.    3. Pablo me dijo que no tirara de ese cable hasta que él

me lo dijera.    4. La enfermera me dijo que esperara allí hasta que me llamaran por el altavoz.
5. Ella me dijo que no fuera al día siguiente.    6. El profesor nos dijo que hiciéramos esos
ejercicios para la semana siguiente.    7. El profesor nos dijo que no olvidáramos llevar el trabajo
terminado.    8. El policía le dijo a mi amigo que no aparcara tan pegado a la pared.

**9-4**   1. Yo le ordené que no usara mi despacho sin que yo estuviera allí. (O: Yo le prohibí que
usara... )    2. Ella le pidió que pasara y (que) se pusiera cómodo. (O: Ella le invitó a pasar y a
ponerse cómodo.)    3. Él dedujo/calculó que ya eran las seis y añadió que deberían irse.    4. El
ladrón le dijo a su compañero que se metiera en ese/aquel armario, porque venía alguien.    5. Yo
le aconsejé/sugerí (a ella) que no aceptara esas/aquellas condiciones.    6. Él me aconsejó/sugirió
que me matriculara en la universidad.    7. Pablo creía que era posible que ella tuviera que declarar
también. (O: Pablo consideraba posible que ella tuviera que declarar también.)    8. Él me pidió
que cogiera eso/aquello y (que) lo llevara a la biblioteca.

**9-5**   1. ¿Puedes /Podrías /Quieres echarme una mano con la limpieza de los cuartos de baño?    2. ¿Por
qué no cogemos un taxi para ir al centro? (O: Cojamos un taxi para ir al centro.)    3. Mis padres
están pensando en el divorcio.    4. Mi marido ha tenido que dejar la empresa porque hay asuntos
sucios.    5. Antonio debe de tener más de cuarenta años. (O: Antonio tiene que tener más de
cuarenta años.)    6. ¡Callaos de inmediato! ¡Estoy intentando estudiar para mañana!    7. No
olvides ir a echar las cartas al correo.    8. ¿Puedes/Podrías/Quieres sujetarme la puerta, por favor?

**9-6**   1. I suggested that they not go to that neighborhood.    2. Mónica advised me to stay a few
days.    3. Paco asked us to take him home, because he wasn't feeling very good.    4. My mother
has forbidden me to see you.    5. My father has promised me that he will take me to the zoo this
weekend.    6. Jaime told them not to come in without taking off their shoes first.    7. I
congratulated them on the birth of their daughter.    8. Manolo told us that his wife was going to
have an operation the next day.    9. I asked them if they had ever eaten in that restaurant.
10. Sara begged us to help her convince her husband.

**9-7**   1. Ella me dijo que no hiciera tanto ruido.    2. Él le dijo (a ella) que esperara allí hasta que él
regresara.    3. Le pregunté a Mari si le apetecía cenar conmigo.    4. Él negó haber escrito esa
carta.    5. Juan se negó a tomar parte en la broma.    6. Ella me ordenó que limpiara el suelo.
7. Miguel sugirió que visitáramos esa ciudad.    8. Él nos aconsejó que no fuéramos allí en coche/
auto.    9. Él nos prohibió que habláramos durante el examen.    10. Ella dijo que no estuvo/había
estado allí el día antes/anterior.

# 10   Problematic prepositions I

**10-1**   1. A    2. a    3. A    4. en    5. en    6. a    7. A    8. a    9. en    10. En

**10-2**   1. Correct    2. bueno contando (*No preposition with gerunds.*)    3. en (la) Navidad    4. A qué
altura    5. a unos doscientos    6. Correct    7. Correct    8. en la boda    9. en la cena    10. Correct

**10-3**   1. en, en/los    2. en, los, por    3. de, a    4. por, al    5. por, en/a    6. en/los, en/-    7. en/-, en
8. en, -    9. en el, en    10. a, en

# 11   Problematic prepositions II

**11-1**   1. a/hacia    2. a    3. para/hacia/-    4. -    5. bajo    6. sobre    7. por/a través de(l)    8. encima/en lo
alto    9. por debajo de    10. por

**11-2**     1. en coche     2. Correct     3. por debajo de ella     4. en/durante el almuerzo     5. Correct
6. Correct     7. Atravesamos un bosquecillo. (O: Fuimos a través de un bosquecillo.)     8. encima
del mío/sobre el mío     9. Correct     10. Correct

**11-3**     1. bajo     2. debajo de/bajo     3. en lo alto del/encima del     4. al     5. a     6. hacia el     7. a
8. a/para     9. dentro de     10. en/durante

# 12   Idiomatic constructions

**12-1**     1. perder la cabeza     2. costar caro     3. pasó canutas     4. lleva camino     5. tonto del bote
6. corta/parte el bacalao     7. tienes/te hace falta abuela     8. buscar una aguja en un pajar

**12-2**     1. las pasó canutas     2. perdió la cabeza     3. se busca/gana la vida     4. han tirado la casa por la
ventana     5. Lo pasé bomba.     6. me da una de cal y otra de arena     7. Estoy haciendo el
agosto.     8. ¡Acabáramos!

**12-3**     1. por casa     2. abrir boca     3. Correct     4. de bote en bote     5. una de cal y otra de arena     6. en
el blanco     7. Correct     8. de baja

**12-4**     1. hizo un lío     2. muerdas la lengua (o: vayas de la lengua)     3. dando largas     4. dar la lata
5. va a parar     6. haciendo aguas     7. donde los haya     8. vayamos al grano

**12-5**     1. como quien oye llover     2. Pablo se fue de la lengua     3. me está dando la lata     4. esto va para
largo     5. dio a luz a gemelos     6. te la han jugado     7. vale un imperio     8. tienen/traen en jaque a
la policía

**12-6**     1. dado en el clavo     2. limar asperezas     3. morderme la lengua     4. Correct     5. Correct
6. empinando el codo     7. Correct     8. hice un lío